the boy he left behind

ALSO BY MARK MATOUSEK

Sex Death Enlightenment (1996)

RIVERHEAD BOOKS

A MEMBER OF

PENGUIN PUTNAM INC.

NEW YORK

2 0 0 0

the
boy
he
left
behind

mark matousek

a

man's

search

for

his

lost

father

Certain names and identifying characteristics of individuals portrayed
in this book have been changed to protect their privacy.

"Father and Son," copyright 1944 by Stanley Kunitz, from *The Poems of
Stanley Kunitz 1928–1978* by Stanley Kunitz. Reprinted by permission
of W. W. Norton & Company, Inc.

RIVERHEAD BOOKS
a member of
Penguin Putnam Inc.
375 Hudson Street
New York, NY 10014

Library of Congress Cataloging-in-Publication Data

Matousek, Mark.
The boy he left behind : a man's search for his lost father / Mark Matousek.
p.   cm.
ISBN 1-57322-154-6
1. Fathers—United States.   2. Fatherhood—Psychological aspects.
3. Fathers and sons—United States.   4. Divorced fathers—United States—
Family relationships.   I. Title.
HQ756.M359   2000   99-054721 CIP
306.874'2—dc21

Printed in the United States of America
1   3   5   7   9   10   8   6   4   2
This book is printed on acid-free paper. ∞

Book design by Claire Naylon Vaccaro

FOR MY MOTHER, IDA MATOUJEK

1926-1994

The deepest search in life, it seemed to me, the thing that in one way or another was central to all living, was man's search to find a father, not merely the father of his flesh, not merely the lost father of his youth, but the image of a strength and wisdom external to his need and superior to his hunger, to which the belief and power of his own life could be united.

THOMAS WOLFE

You will begin to forgive the world when you forgive your father.

TENNESSEE WILLIAMS'S
PSYCHIATRIST

· one ·

I was four years old when my father came back to kidnap me. It was Sunday night, Ed Sullivan night, the TV was blasting, and I was making so much noise that we didn't hear his truck drive up. This is how my sisters tell it. Mom was next door playing calookie, Joyce was sacked out on the couch, Marcia was cross-legged on the floor, bouncing Belle in her lap. "A really big *shoe!*" I was screaming at Ed's ugly mortician's face, swinging my body back and forth like a two-by-four with arms nailed on.

When he gunned the motor I ran to the window, and seconds later the room was in chaos. Marcia blocked the door, Joyce tore past us into the kitchen. I tried to squeeze between Marcia's legs, but she locked her knees around my head. Joyce screamed for Mom through the window. Then my father banged on the door and told me to open up.

"Don't be scared, son. I'm not gonna hurt you."

Marcia clamped my mouth shut with the palm of her hand. I bit her hard. She gave me a wallop.

"Hurry up!" he said.

"Mommy said no," Marcia told him.

"Then get yourselves out of the way!"

His first kick did nothing but shake the wall. The second kick put my father's boot right through the bottom of the door. Marcia screamed and let me go—I lunged for the knob and turned it. My father grabbed me and ran for the truck, hoisting me up like I weighed nothing. I was naked to the waist and barefoot. I remember my father panting and clutching my ribs, rubbing my cheek raw against his face. In the hot night air, he smelled like smoke and mayonnaise.

We were next to the truck when I heard Mom scream. I turned and saw her running toward us, shrieking nasty words. Her hair was in curlers, her face deranged. Then I felt her hands on my ankles, yanking me hard till my father lost his grip and I was stretched out tight between them, belly up, being pulled apart. I yelled at them but they wouldn't stop. They snarled and spat like crazy dogs, thrashing and barking and showing their teeth. I bit my tongue and my mouth filled with blood; puke clogged the back of my throat. Then she kicked him hard in the basket.

The next thing I knew, I was over Mom's shoulder, and she was running toward the house. "I'm locking you up!" she screamed at my father, then slammed the door and started shaking. "Don't even try it!" Joyce said when I struggled to get past her to the door. Marcia was sobbing with Belle in her arms. Mom was on the phone to the cops, telling them to come and arrest my father. I screamed through the window but he couldn't hear me.

"Wait!" I pounded the glass with my fists. Joyce pinned my arms behind my back. My father was bent double over the hood. Then he straightened up, opened the car door, slid inside, gunned the motor. He sat a minute and honked the horn once, then inched back out of the driveway. The headlights bounced when the truck hit the street, then disappeared slowly down the block.

I never saw or heard from my father again.

· two ·

Thirty-two years later, I'm sitting in a restaurant in lower Manhattan, feeling shaky. I see my reflection in three mirrors opposite—bullet-faced, beaky-nosed, suddenly old—with wisps of hair feathered over the bald spots. I straighten my tie and try to look normal, puff out my cheeks, stare at the door. Why do editors have to be late? Why does lateness simulate power? I glance at the watch of the woman at the table next to mine. Five more minutes, and I'm walking out.

When Joe arrives, he checks out the room and motions the maitre d' toward my seat. He's dressed in a two-thousand-dollar suit, the color of Italian plums, and thick, black, smart-people glasses. His hair is buzzed, his boots are polished, and when he hugs me, my lips touch silk.

"So?" Joe asks, "what's new and exciting?" What he really means is, *please don't bore me.* Joe's preternaturally bored these days—it comes with the job—but he's also goodhearted and extremely loyal. When we first became friends, in the mid-nineteen-eighties, I was a senior editor at *Interview* magazine, Andy Warhol's pop monthly, and Joe was the struggling freelance drone. Now, I'm the one on the outside, begging. Every few months, when I run out of money, I come to Joe with story ideas and he writes me out a handful of contracts.

Once we've ordered and settled in, I pitch him the usual list of harebrained proposals. Every time he nods his head, another month of my rent gets paid.

"Thanks," I say.

"You're welcome," he says. When Joe takes off his glasses to rub his eyes, I see how completely exhausted he is. This is when I remember we're buddies, seeing the damage behind the chic. "It's going so fast," he says, meaning life.

"It is," I say. "It really is."

"We're almost forty. How sick is that?"

"Very sick."

"You're telling me."

Over the years, we've shared lots of secrets. I've borrowed Joe's apartment, smoked his dope, packed up his dishes when he's moved, helped him navigate through bad romances. One afternoon in the wilds of Montauk, we skinny-dipped in frigid green water while my friend Barbara watched us and shivered. I'd like to tell Joe my troubles now, but I'm afraid of saying too much, like a drunk in a bar, revealing more than he wants to know. So I keep them to myself.

Lunch comes fast, our moods start to lighten; we turn our attention to overpriced pasta and gossip about all the people we know. We talk about sex and how women are smarter about it than we are. We talk about hair growing out of our ears; Joe lifts his coat and pinches his love handles, telling me they're now a permanent fixture. I assure him that he's never looked better, but Joe shakes his head like I'm out of my mind.

"You're even becoming a star," I say. Walking past Barneys several months back, I'd stopped to look in the department store's Father's Day window and seen a poster of Joe and his dad sitting shirtless together on a bench. I tell Joe his father looks like a nice guy.

"He rode my ass when I was a kid."

"What about now?"

"We get along. Barely."

"He lives in New York?"

"Across the Hudson," Joe says. "Close enough. What about yours?"

"We have no contact."

"Why not?" he asks.

"You don't want to know."

It's odd that we've never discussed our families but I hate this story and rarely tell it. Not that it hurts me—it honestly doesn't. I hardly remember my father's face, and my feelings for him have long since scarred over. Now and then, when he crosses my mind—or rather, his ghost floats back for a second—there's nothing left but leathery numbness, like skin that's been frozen to excise a wart. But Joe insists on knowing the details. Factually and as briefly as possible, I tell him about the botched kidnapping, aware as I speak of how neutral I sound, like a writer describing a distant event. It's become a third-person story now: the man in the truck, the crying woman; even the boy with his face at the window no longer has any relation to me. When I finish talking, my throat feels dry; other than that, it's conversation.

"That's what happened."

"And *then?*" asks Joe.

"Then nothing."

"Nothing?"

"Zero."

"Dead?"

"Who knows."

"Didn't you ever look for him?"

I shake my head.

"Why not?"

"Why would I?"

He gives me the pitying look I know well from years of telling people this tale. It's as though you've said that your dog was run over, or the bump on your head is, in fact, malignant. Suddenly you're a charity case.

"Strange," he says.

"Why strange?"

"Because this is your father you're talking about."

"That doesn't mean a thing to me."

"Uh huh."

"Uh huh *what?*"

"Nothing." For a moment, Joe glances around the room as if allowing the subject to drop. Then he leans forward and says, "I think you should look for him."

"No."

"I dare you."

7

"That's crazy."

"You're scared."

"I'm not scared!"

"Of course you're scared. Anyone would be."

Every time he says the word *scared,* I feel myself getting more agitated. As coolly as I can, I say, "I'm just not interested."

"Right," says Joe. He's tapping his coffee spoon, watching me squirm. "I can see that."

"Stop."

"You want to. It's obvious."

"I wasn't the son that he wanted," I say, wishing instantly that I hadn't.

"Let me guess. Your mother said that."

"So what?"

"Then why did he come back for you?"

"He didn't know who I was yet."

"Oh, my God have you been brainwashed."

"It's true."

"Yeah, right."

"You don't understand the situation."

But Joe doesn't buy it—he thinks I'm lying. I know the reporter's code, the way he's smirking and egging me on. He thinks I'm a patsy, a pussy-whipped son. He thinks that my story's a cover-up. If the tables were turned, I might even agree. But they're not, I'm not in the mood, and besides, this is ancient history. I look at Joe's watch and pretend that I have somewhere to go. He calls the waiter for the bill.

"You know what I think?"

"I know what you think, Joe."

"You have to try. It's settled."

"It's not and I don't."

"You have no choice."

"Of course I do."

"There's nothing to lose."

"There's always something to lose," I say.

Joe ignores this and pays the bill. On the sidewalk outside, he tells me to go home and give it some thought. A half hour later, I play back a message from Joe's secretary, giving me the phone number and address of a private detective.

· three ·

I'm at my desk a few days later, just before dawn, trying to work. Below my window, the courtyard is half-dark, children's toys scattered among the rose bushes. My garbage tree, which is what we call sycamores in New York, rises up thirty feet from the garden, its bare limbs reaching over the top of my window. Christmas is past and the branches are cracking; two turtledoves, close to the tree trunk, twist their necks round each other and peck. To the left of the building, the gray stucco wall of the Church of St. John blocks my view of Christopher Street, enclosing this room in surprising quiet. A stained-glass window depicts the Ascension. The chimes I've hung from the fire escape, sounding now in the late fall breeze, remind me of the bazaar where I found them, in the Himalayan town of Leh.

Louis is under the covers, snoring. We live together in these two small rooms without even a door between them. There's a single closet, a roach-ridden kitchen, a bright tiny bathroom. Before Louis moved in last month, the place was even more ascetic: a single towel, a fork, a plate, a knife, one pair of battered blue jeans, tennis shoes, a jacket, a futon; everything in singular, worn beyond the point of comfort. This metal desk from the Salvation Army, a straight-backed chair, and a threadbare loveseat found on the sidewalk, carried upstairs with the help of a homeless man into whose pocket I slipped five dollars. When Louis first saw my humble surroundings, he seemed a little uncomfortable, but Spartan decor doesn't bother me. Since moving back to New York last year, I've grown to love this little place, vermin and all. I've thought of it as my monk's cell in the crotch of Babylon. Louis has added a few creature comforts—a TV set, a stereo, an Art Deco chair that belongs in Miami—but mostly he's learned to live at my level, with admirably little complaint.

When the sun clears the building, it blinds me for a second. Louis tramps into the bathroom to pee. I can't seem to focus on writing today—the message from Joe is still in my mind. I even dreamt of my mother last night. She was curled up on the street like a hobo, ankles swollen, holding up a filthy palm covered, it seemed, with motor grease. She had a bandanna around her head, and one of her eyes was all white, blind-looking like that of a wall-eyed horse. I didn't even stop to help her; instead I ran as fast as I could down the street, fists in my pockets. When I woke up sobbing, Louis held me under the blanket. His breast is as soft as a woman's sometimes. I'm not quite used to this tenderness yet.

When I first told Louis that I was a loner who'd recently led a nomadic life, he asked me what I was running from. We'd met a few days earlier in the flower shop where he works; now we were sitting across a red-checked tablecloth, eating lasagna, trying to bond on our first date. Louis didn't like to talk, but when he spoke, he meant what he said.

"What are you running from?" he repeated when I told him that, in the past six years, I'd lived in twenty-six different locations. The question insulted me. I wasn't running, I was a seeker; there was a difference. The way I saw it, seekers were heroes, while running was a cowardly act. After the plague struck and friends started dying, I quit my job as an editor and shifted gears from struggling up the media ladder to making sense of what, if anything, life might *mean*. I wanted to know why I felt inauthentic, as if I were a chronic impostor; why, in spite of an outwardly prosperous life, I was so drained and depressed inside, and sometimes even wanted to die. I knew that my soul needed careful attention whether my body was sick or not, and I spent the next six years seeking answers and training from teachers and priests, traveling in Europe and India, immersing myself in spiritual texts, believing that only a higher power could fill this grim emptiness inside me. This seeking became more focused and urgent the day I learned I had the virus. Louis listened to all this without reacting, then quietly said that three months before, he'd woken up to find his partner of nine years dead on the pillow beside him. Louis didn't flinch when he said it, adding that he was infected as well. It took me a minute to catch my breath. Then he asked how I'd come to believe that meaning was something that one had to search for, as if one's essence, one's *life*, were elsewhere.

"I'm talking about enlightenment," I said, thinking that he didn't understand. "Enlightenment with a capital E."

He looked at me through the flickering candlelight, pausing a long time before he responded. Finally, he asked, "Do you mean kindness?"

Kindness, indeed, I wanted to spit—as if the glories of philosophy could be reduced so plainly! I wanted to put Louis in his place; instead, I shut my caustic mouth and felt completely humiliated. Clearly Louis had hit a nerve, seeing through my sacred blather to the heart of something I did not want to admit. Somehow, in all my compulsive seeking, I'd forgotten that enlightenment started with love. The words I mouthed were abstractions— in truth—wisdom was simpler and closer to hand. I saw that Louis could teach me something I hadn't been ready to learn before and, six weeks later, with great trepidation, I asked him if he would live with me.

Now, as Louis turns on the shower, I stare out the window. Across the way, a balding man is standing by his kitchen sink, wearing only his boxer shorts. A foot-long scar runs the length of his abdomen, like purple train tracks from neck to navel. How would it feel to be laid on a table, cracked open, and put back together? How would it feel to be split in half, then wake up knowing your heart had been changed? And why haven't I ever looked for my father? Why, in the dream, did I run past my mother, and wake up feeling so bereft? Why is part of me always gone, always elsewhere, on the lam, and what is this phantom part really seeking? I thought it was God, a transcendent embrace, but now I've begun to have my doubts. In spite of all I've learned and seen, this hunger has hardly decreased at all. I still feel a fugitive in my own life, chasing something I never quite catch. But what is this dog in my heart, I wonder, and what precisely is it chasing?

· four ·

In a wood-paneled office overlooking Broadway, the detective leans across his desk with a big, pink outstretched hand. "Mac Sullivan!" he announces. "Have a seat! This place is a shithole. When you gonna clean this place up, Liz?"

The secretary who showed me in looks at him cross-eyed.

"She looks smart but up here," he tells me, tapping his snowy-haired temple, "Play-Doh."

"Can I bring you some coffee?" she asks me.

"Yeah, can she get you some coffee?" Sullivan is sitting on the edge of the desk in front of me, dangling a perfectly pleated leg. "Or how about an Evian?"

"I'll take an Evian."

"The man wants an Evian," he taunts her. This must be their routine for new clients. Sullivan reaches behind him for a book and hands it to me. It's a glossy bestseller about a recent major corporate shakedown. "That was my project," Sullivan says, producing a résumé that features the names of corporate titans and ex-presidents. Modesty is obviously not his style.

When the secretary comes back with my water and his black coffee, Sullivan sits behind his desk and picks up a yellow legal pad. I take out my tape recorder.

"You mind?" I ask.

"Why should I mind?"

"Some people do."

"I've got nothing to hide."

I fumble with the microcassette and finally get the spindle to turn. Sullivan's tapping the desk with a lacquered fingernail. "So, you want to find your father," he asks.

"I think so."

"You think so?"

"No, I do."

He looks sideways at me, wondering if I'm wasting his time.

"I called you on the spur of the moment."

"Maybe you should think it over."

"No need."

"These things can get messy."

"I realize that."

"All right then, let's get down to business." Sullivan picks up his pen. "You've looked for him before?"

"Never."

"Why now?"

"That's complicated." Sullivan looks skeptical again, as if I'm being deliberately cagey, but truthfully I don't know what to tell him. I called because Joe dared me to, and other friends pushed me onto the bandwagon? I called because his number was there? I called because I'm thirty-six, the same age my father was when he left, and waiting for the ax to fall? Motivation's a complex thing, I'd like to say to this blustery man. Things don't happen for clear-cut reasons. Instead, I simply tell him, "It's time."

"No pressing reason? No money involved? No death in the family?"

"It just seems like something I should do."

"Sort of a lark?"

"Sort of," I say.

"Whatever blows your hair back," he says. I can tell by the titter in Sullivan's voice that he's now half-convinced I'm a flake. He asks me a series of questions about my father's vital statistics, most of which I cannot answer. Since my mother never met her in-laws, I know nothing at all about my paternal family, except that they came from Illinois. My father was homeless when she first met him, working as a fix-it man in the boarding house where she was living, and aside from the barest physical description—tall, skinny, gray eyes, a cleft in his chin that could hold a quarter—I know nothing.

"Last seen?" asks Sullivan.

"June, 1961."

"Documents? Marriage certificate?"

"Somewhere. Maybe."

"They *were* married?"

"Apparently."

"Photographs? Of him, I mean."

"Not anymore." I had a photo of my father once, a wallet-smashed black-and-white snapshot I used to squint at when I was a kid, trying to make out his face. He was standing next to Mom, in a short-sleeved plaid shirt. His hands were planted on Marcia's shoulders, Joyce was missing her front teeth, everyone was smiling big. Mom was pregnant with me. The photo disappeared years ago.

"Child support?"

"Not a penny."

"How many kids?"

"Four. Two were his."

"Your mother struggled?"

"Hard," I say.

"I'm gonna get this son of a bitch."

"I don't want anything from him," I say.

"Well, I'd like to see his ass in jail." I notice that Sullivan's color is rising; this seems to have touched a personal chord. I don't want to see my father in jail—I'm not sure that I want to see him at all. But since I'm convinced that this won't happen—how could it possibly on such a whim?—I don't bother dousing Sullivan's aggression.

He puts down his notepad and caps his pen. "That's good enough for a start," he tells me. "Now it's time to squeeze your mother for more information."

"Believe me, I've tried."

"Squeeze again," he says.

· five ·

The detective doesn't know what he's asking. The prospect of letting my mother in on this search, let alone probing her with questions, is both frightening and futile. Though I've earned my living doing interviews for the past fifteen years, persuading public figures to spit out their secrets in print, my skills are worthless with Ida. She isn't a person who likes to look back; the past, in her eyes, is a place to escape from, a haunting reminder of loss and regret. After decades of trying to learn her secrets, I've long since given up and allowed our relationship to dwindle. Every few weeks, I call her collect from wherever I am to confirm that we're both still vertical and breathing. Once a year, sometimes less, I make the tense journey home, glad to see Belle and her three sons, dreading time spent alone with Mom. Whenever the two of us are marooned together, the scene is always the same: ten minutes of small talk followed by long stretches of strangled silence. I'm forbidden from trying to fill this dead air with anything vaguely provocative. I talk about the rain in New York; she talks about the price of brisket. We cover our nervousness with sighs and feel the same embarrassed relief when our solitude is at last interrupted by one of Belle's sons, or my own sudden need for a walk. It's agonizing trying to talk to my mother, like dancing with a burn victim. There's nowhere to touch her that won't make her flinch.

It's Sunday afternoon when I call, a few days after meeting Mac Sullivan. My mother is potchkying in the kitchen, TV blaring in the background. Her voice is even deeper than usual, slowed down by vodka and orange juice. Mom started drinking when Marcia died. She always sounded butch on the phone. Now she sounds like Ernest Borgnine.

"So," she says.

"So," I say.

"You're good?"

"I'm fine. And you?"

"Fine."

"That's good."

"Status quo," she says, running water, clinking utensils. "So what can I do you for?"

"You'll never believe what happened," I say.

"What's wrong?"

"Nothing's wrong." She always expects the worst. "I just decided to do something funny."

"Yeah?"

"For the hell of it. As a joke."

She covers the phone and shouts something to Bruce, her live-in boyfriend of fifteen years. "He's making me crazy." Then to me, "Tell me, I'm listening."

"I hired a guy to look for my father." I say it fast before I can back out.

My mother says nothing, not a peep. I hear cheering from a football game, and heavy, sporadic breathing.

"Mom?"

No response.

"Talk to me."

"What do you want me to say?" she asks.

"It's not like I'm going to find him."

"He's dead."

"I know that. Probably."

"He *is*," she insists.

"How do you know?"

"I know." Her voice drops from baritone to bass. After murdering my father in her mind all these years, she can't stomach the fact that he may have survived.

"Wouldn't you like to find out for sure?"

Another extended, howling silence.

"I'd like to know."

"So know," she says. "I'm hanging up."

"If you hang up this phone I'm not calling back."

She doesn't hang up.

"I don't understand what the big deal is," I go on.

"I want you to leave this alone," she says.

"I don't want to leave it alone. I need to ask you some questions," I say.

Her lighter clicks. She sucks on her smoke.

"Mom? Please."

No response.

"When were you married?"

"I don't remember."

"Where was the wedding?"

"I don't remember."

"What were his parents' names?"

"How the hell should I know."

"Brothers and sisters?"

"If you don't stop."

"Okay," I say, surprised that she's allowed me to get this far. "Just tell me one more thing."

"What do you *want* from me?"

"Why don't you want me to find him? Really. If he was alive?"

At first she says nothing—I fear I've pushed too hard. Then she says quietly, "You couldn't take it."

"Maybe I could."

"Well, maybe I couldn't."

So that's it, I think, the real bottom line.

"Just one more thing and I'll leave you alone." Since my mother works downtown in City Hall, I ask her to stop by the Hall of Records and request a copy of the marriage certificate. She tells me to go jump in the lake, which means, in her language, that she'll do it.

My sister Belle is thrilled by the news. "I don't believe it!" she screams above the bedlam of toddlers she baby-sits at her home daycare center in the Antelope Valley. Belle was only a year old in 1961 and grew up without the dubious comfort of knowing that her father wanted her enough to try to snatch her away in the night. She used to cry a lot as a girl on the rare occasions his name was mentioned, and pined in a way that I did not for a man she doesn't remember at all.

"Please don't get your hopes up," I say.

"I can't believe he could meet my kids!"

"He could meet us."

"It's too strange. Mom would die."

"She already did." I tell Belle about my conversation with Ida. "Are you scared?"

"I'm numb," I tell her. It's true. I have no idea what I should be feeling. *Father* means nothing but absence to me; the word itself is a kind of black hole, sucking up what's familiar around it. It leaves me feeling mute and disjointed.

"Well, I think it's fantastic," Belle says.

"He's probably dead."

"You sound just like Mom."

"I don't want you to get too excited."

"Too late," she tells me. "I already am."

· six ·

I become the Matousek Matter. That's the heading on the first of the hundred or so memos that start arriving from Mac Sullivan's office, keeping me abreast of his every move. The documents report a nationwide paper chase involving banks, Social Security locators, the Department of Motor Vehicles, telephone book searches, the National Look Up Service, library scans, computer surname identifiers, and other organs to track missing persons— with what little information we have. In addition to these legitimate venues, Sullivan confides on the phone that he's using ulterior sources as well, assuring me that many people in high places owe him favors.

"Back alleys," Sullivan says. "That's where the garbage turns up."

I wince at his word choice.

"I don't mean that your father's garbage."

"Right," I say.

"You just need to know the ins and outs."

"Of course."

"I'm telling you, I'm the best."

Once the lists start piling in, I'm amazed to discover how many people, dead and alive, have my father's name. There are dozens of James Matouseks scattered across the country, the highest concentration being in the Midwest, where Czechs immigrated in vast numbers around the turn of the century. I carefully study these photocopied listings, each accompanied by an address and statistics, half-expecting one of them to jump out at me. I can scarcely believe that my father's number may actually be staring me in the face—that James M. in Cicero, Illinois, or James H. in Hennessey, Oklahoma, could actually be the one, an eleven-digit dial away.

And what would I do if he picked up the phone? What in the name of God would I say? With Sullivan's lists spread out before me, the prospect seems almost feasible. Closing my eyes, I freefall back in search of my father's voice, but can grasp not so much as an echo. I try to imagine him saying my name but it's just me talking back to myself. How would I approach him, I wonder? Like a long-pursued interview subject? The biggest interview of my life with someone impossibly hard to track down—Jim Matousek as Mr. Kurtz, the mysterious guy from *Heart of Darkness,* sitting on all the answers in his African outpost. After years of beating my way through a jungle of rumors, propaganda, fictions, and lies, I imagine standing in front of this stranger armed with five essential questions. What would those questions possibly be? I reach for a pen, then write down the following without thinking. *Why did you leave me? Where did you go? How does a man act? Am I good? How should I live now?*

These queries appear automatically, as if they'd already been formed. This question of whether I'm good or not—and the other four issues, too, in their way—echoes the questions I've put to teachers I've met along the dharma trail. It seems odd that I would be moved to make these same inquiries of my father, as if James Matousek, whoever he is, were some sort of priest in my subconscious. Superstitious as this appears, the connection intrigues me nonetheless.

I turn my eyes to a black-and-white portrait I keep on my desk. In the photo, I'm sitting with a Christian mystic known as the Magus of Strovolos—or simply as Daskalos (The Teacher)—to his thousands of students around the world. We'd just completed our interview, and the eighty-year-old holy man from Cyprus is leaning forward, holding my hand and smiling, craggy-faced, in a cardigan sweater. I look electrified and nervous. His entourage had already dispersed, and only the two of us were left in the hotel room with my friend Paula, who'd come to take photos. I'd wanted to ask for some word of advice, but before I could say anything, the old man looked straight at me and said in a heavy accent, "You are good." Three simple words—just that—but when he said them I wanted to cry. I choke up whenever I think of that moment, and the piercing sense I had in his sanctified presence of being accepted as I was—and seen—with love free of judgment. Looking at this image now, I'm uncomfortable and a little confused that the question I'd like to ask my father echoes this holy man's words so precisely.

Turning from this photograph to the scene outside my window, I notice something unusual on the silver-painted roof next door, a large black boot in the far corner that seems to have dropped out of nowhere. It looks sinister at the angle it's landed, on its side with the mouth stretched open—tongue wagging, laces trailing like the innards of a shot-down crow. Abandoned shoes remind me of death whenever I come across them outdoors, as if they'd just been stepped out of by ghosts. Today, with a charcoal sky overhead and rain beginning to fall on the rooftop, the big black boot looks especially ominous and totemic. It conjures a dead man who's walked away and left a dark empty mouth behind him. I make a note to have it removed.

· seven ·

My mother cried when I was born. That's what she told me when I was a child. Hearing the word *boy* through her twilight sleep, this woman who never did anything right, felt, for a moment, that she just had. She thought that a son might be a good omen, born to turn her luck around. A boy might settle the war inside her, hold up the roof of a house that was falling. I used to conjure this scene in my mind, picture my mother's tears of joy when the doctor laid me on top of her and my father rushed in to see his first-born son, then touched my reddened face with his fingers as I nuzzled against her breast.

This is how I liked to see it, looking back at how I was born, though later I realized that this was a fiction. In fact, their marriage didn't stand a chance—a dozen boy children could not have healed it. My parents were both unmarriageable, lost souls, out-casts, runaways, scrambling to get on track. They'd come together out of defeat and grabbed each other for all the wrong reasons. I couldn't change this, nor had I caused it, but as a boy I feared that I had and needed to think that my birth at least had brought a moment of authentic joy to an otherwise hopeless affair.

This was in 1957. Smog hardly existed in L.A. then. Ike and Mamie were in the White House, men used Brylcreem, the country was booming. Buicks were 18.9 feet long. The San Fernando Valley, where we lived, was still largely farmland, orange groves and acres of corn where the freeways and strip malls stand today. The natural light there was so painterly that film directors came thousands of miles to capture what cinematographers called the "magic moment" at sunset, when North Hollywood turned into Shangri-la. There could hardly have been a better time to be thirty years old and showgirl pretty in the new American West, but my mother's life was already in shambles.

Making trouble came naturally to her. From the time that she was a little girl working in Grandpa's dairy store—on Pelham Parkway, in the Bronx—candling eggs and cutting cheese, Ida was the problem child, the second daughter who should have been a son. The knowledge that she was the wrong sex, at least in her immigrant father's eyes, twisted my mother early on. She could hardly compete with my Aunt Ruth, her sweet-faced older sister, who'd be cuddled upstairs in Grandma's bed while Ida hauled pails of milk for Grandpa. She seems, almost from birth, to have felt locked out of both worlds—the arena of women, the tribe of men—and concluded that since she was such a misfit, she might as well start acting like one.

Grandpa had come on a boat from Russia when he was eighteen, and earned enough money sorting buttons at a factory on

Delancey Street to support his four younger brothers and a tyrant father whom he despised. Grandpa wasn't a bad man, just a miser who'd been convinced by his *shtetl* childhood that the big bad world was out to rob him. He taught the daughter he wished was a son how to swindle and compete. "Take them before they take you, Eye," he used to tell my mother, "that's the American way." He taught her how to water down milk and fudge the scale weights— subtle maneuvers to cheat their customers and bolster profits. Then he'd send her off in the dark to deliver to neighbors who knew that Sid Kaplan jacked up his prices, but who had no other kosher store on the block.

Grandma Bella had come from a village in Poland six years before Ruth was born, then worked in a sweatshop stringing human hair through the acrylic skulls of dolls. Resting the plastic heads in her lap, she asked herself—as she later told my Aunt Ruth—what kind of normal boy would want a girl barely five feet tall. When she first saw Grandpa at a mixer on Orchard Street, Bella told herself that if she could love a boy with elephant ears, he could love a dainty girl. When she suspected that Sid didn't know how to love, and realized later that he never would, Bella comforted herself with the thought that the love she felt was enough for them both. In the eighteen months after their modest wedding, she bore him two dark-skinned, big-eyed daughters.

Ida was willful from the start. Perhaps because Ruth was so eager to please, my mother seemed just as eager not to. "Rules were made to be broken," she told me as far back as I can remember (though she'd come to regret this later on when I couldn't stay out of jail). The more impeccable Ruthie was, getting good grades and spit-curling her hair, the more of a hellion Ida became. While her sister was in the kitchen helping Grandma stuff kishka, pushing cornmeal into cow entrails with a wire hanger, Ida would be stealing perfume at the drugstore or smoking cigarettes with the Italians. Aunt Ruth says that my mother always had a destructive streak, and when puberty hit, Ida's body became her instrument of emotional ruin. Between the ages of ten and thirteen, nature transformed a narrow-hipped tomboy into a kind of local sex goddess, with the sass and curves of a chorus girl. Her male friends in the neighborhood—and then their brothers, uncles, and fathers—couldn't wait to get a look at Ida Kaplan's chest, or a feel, which they copped every chance they could, with or without her consent. "They wouldn't leave me alone," Mom would tell me, sounding equally bitter and proud. Sadly, she learned to crave this attention, to think of herself as a big-bosomed broad, a walking Touch Me sign for any horny man with fingers. Underneath her trampy ways, though, she had the soul of a stricken romantic, and convinced herself that one of these dogs would actually fall in love with her.

None did. This was the early nineteen-forties, and very few respectable men wanted to love a girl like that for more than twenty minutes. Grandma Bella wrung her hands as she watched Ida throw herself away, but when she tried to reason with her, telling Ida to save herself for a husband, my mother just laughed and did as she pleased. On a family outing to Coney Island when she was fifteen, Ida puffed out her chest and tossed her hair like Sophia Loren in a cinch-waisted skirt, drawing wolf whistles from the men on the boardwalk. Then she turned to Grandma Bella— hook-nosed, four-feet-ten, wearing orthopedic sandals and a flowered housedress—and asked, without a hint of shame, how it felt to have a daughter as beautiful as she was.

"Beauty fades," Grandma told her, but Ida didn't want to believe it. When Grandpa padlocked her bedroom door, my mother strapped on her high heels and snuck down the fire escape into the tattooed arms of one of her favorite thugs. "I always went for the bad boys," she'd tell me after her looks were gone and my father had long since run off. It was hard for me as a little boy to picture this stony-faced woman, with her chewed-down nails and short hair combed like a man's, as ever having been pretty and young, but the high school portrait she kept in the shadow box proved that she had indeed been a beauty. Even today when I look at this photo, yellowed on my desk as I write this, two inches square and creased through her nose, it requires a leap of imagination to link that pretty teenage face to the battered visage I grew up with.

Battered. That's the only word that truly describes the damage I saw in my mother's face. She looked for violent men to love; rough men excited her. Ida was rough herself and needed men who could make her feel soft, men who were tougher and meaner than she was. That's the erotic explanation for why she felt drawn to lowlifes and brutes. The deeper truth is that Mom was ashamed, hated herself, and felt undeserving of tenderness. Sex and bravado were masks for failure. She'd failed, first of all, by not being a boy, then failed as a daughter, sister, student; now she'd fail as a lover and wife by seeking men who were bound to hurt her. I know that this happened; I've heard all the rumors. I heard Grandpa call her a whore and a slut, and though I barely knew what those words meant at five or six, they stuck in my mind alongside *chazars*, pigs in Yiddish, Grandpa's word for the men my mother snuck out to be with, who'd done such terrible things to her. I can visualize the dark parking lot, three men in a car, and my mother trapped. I can see a hand clamped over her mouth, her foot on the headrest, a radio cranked up to deafening volume so passersby can't hear the struggle (it's a summer night, the windows are open). I picture thick fingertips ripping her nipples, greasers in the front seat laughing, taking turns, pinning her head back, the scene dragging on for hours till my mother's face is the color of cardboard.

I can't pinpoint where these images come from, but this is a story that I've known forever, and written about in journals and fiction. The details are fuzzy, the essence isn't: something brutal happened to her. Something scared her into wanting to change. She realized that her game was out of control, that playing this way could get her killed. She stopped sneaking out at night, studied enough to graduate from high school, and some time around her eighteenth birthday, after Aunt Ruth had become engaged, decided that she too wanted to start a family. It wasn't easy for her to find a husband, but after nosing around for prospects, my mother came across an overweight kid from the lefty housing projects who knew nothing about her reputation. At two hundred and fifty pounds, with Brillo hair and a voice like a eunuch, Milty Horowitz felt, I imagine, as if the heavens had opened up and dropped a Ziegfeld girl in his lap.

· eight ·

God is a lousy editor sometimes; most people's lives make nonsensical books. If I were rewriting my mother's life I'd do it without the non sequiturs, without the episodes that don't hold water, the characters without depth or purpose, the lack of a focused moral viewpoint. If I could retell my mother's story with God's red pencil in my hand, this is where I'd change direction; right here, on the brink of disaster. I'd substitute a true revelation for Mom's belief as she walked down the aisle that becoming a wife would legitimize her, and having children would give her life meaning. In the enlightened version I'd like to compose, my mother would have confronted her demons—especially her terror of being alone—before the ring was slipped on her finger. She'd have turned from the *chuppah,* the rabbi, the wineglass, and left the synagogue all by herself to find out who she really was, before making vows she could not keep to a man she never loved.

As it was, she married Milty that day with surprisingly high hopes, and moved with him into a tenement flat around the corner from Grandpa's store. Within two years, they had two daughters, first quiet, sad-eyed, lovable Marcia, then chubby, screaming, ornery Joyce, as different from her older sister as Ida was from Ruth. My mother's first stumbling block in this new role was clear to everyone but her: she disliked children immensely. She had no patience for fussing and crying; being *clung* to gave her the willies. She'd assumed that when the children were hers this longtime antipathy would change, but in fact it only grew worse. My sisters' utter dependency, together with Milty's gargantuan lust, felt too much like suffocation. Wherever she turned they were pawing at her the way my mother had been pawed at since she sprouted breasts; and with everyone wanting a piece of her, she withdrew and turned cold in self-defense. Ida wanted to love her daughters the way Aunt Ruth adored her two children, but since she couldn't stand the girls' clamor, or Milty's clumsy attempts at affection, Marcia and Joyce grew up as outsiders.

A child knows its mother's mind; a glance from her, a touch, a word, and all the information she wants, or doesn't want, is passed along in a moment's contact. The girls saw clearly that they weren't wanted, felt the chill that Mom tried to cover, noted her absence as she withdrew. They read the thought behind her eyes— the wish that her daughters had never been born—and my mother's terrible guilt for so wishing. The more they tried to squeeze her for warmth, the more my mother gulped for air. I understand this reflex in her—intimacy can be oppressive. I struggle against this with Louis sometimes when the fact of his need for me feels too intense, his hunger for connection too close. I'm seized by the impulse to run away, certain that I'll never satisfy him, and that I'll fail miserably at this commitment. But my mother could not articulate her fear and instead withdrew automatically, confused by her inability to give. I saw this aversion in her firsthand one day before I was in kindergarten. We were sitting next to the bedroom closet, just the two of us, watching our cat nurse a litter of kittens. Twiggy had rolled over onto her side, paws held up in maternal surrender, staring past us with glazed eyes as ten calico babies clawed at her bloated white belly, each fighting for a nipple. I remember being mesmerized, as if a miracle were occurring there among my mother's stiletto heels, but after a minute Mom left the room. She said she couldn't breathe in there; the nursing kittens made her queasy. I realize now that before I was born she herself had felt pinned to the floor by a ravenous fat man and two needy daughters; and that, to stop from going crazy, she had to find some means of escape.

My mother began with mailmen and milk boys, according to family rumors, then escalated to grocers, hard hats, and taxi drivers. She used the charms that she knew best, and her flirtations soon mushroomed to stolen kisses, a pinch here or there in the doorway or park, a cup of tea when Milty was working, an interlude of afternoon petting when she thought that Marcia and Joyce weren't looking. In time, she began an affair with a neighborhood bigmouth who bragged to his friends till the rumor made its way back to Milty. I can't imagine that Mom was surprised; she always seemed to get caught. "I'm the world's worst liar," she used to tell me, though that is only partly true. When Milty found out about her lover and threatened to confine her as Grandpa had tried to do, my mother fought back like a cat in a cage. After he caught her a second time, and took a belt to her with the girls watching, she fled to her parents' house. Marcia described the welts she'd seen on Mom's legs, and watching Grandma rub chicken fat into the bruises. Bella pleaded with her younger daughter to be a good wife, to think of the children, while Grandpa told Ida that she was no good and deserved whatever she got. Feeling trapped, with no allies to help her, Mom slipped down the tenement stairs one night with Marcia and Joyce—kidnapping her daughters as my father would try to kidnap me—and caught a train to California.

When she arrived in Los Angeles on the Super Chief in the winter of 1956, with her six- and seven-year-old daughters and nobody, but nobody, to tell her what to do, Ida felt that she'd stepped out of hell into a Technicolor dream. The sidewalks were lined with flowers, not slush; the air was sweet with orange blossoms; women with suntans and sunglasses sped by in shiny convertibles. Best of all, my mother thought, there was nobody here who knew who she was, no sordid past for her to live down. She believed she could make a fresh start under powder-blue skies, and live it up while she was still young. Although Aunt Ruth had moved to L.A. the year before with Uncle Marty and their young daughter, she had no extra space with another baby on the way. Instead, my mother found a room at a Fairfax Avenue boarding house for unmarried women and settled the girls in as well as she could, waiting for something good to happen, meaning a man who was more to her taste than the oaf she'd just left behind.

Milty married again soon after their divorce and kept little contact with the girls.

I have no history of my father, not so much as a rumor of where he'd been before the April day he first saw my mother stretched out on a lawn chair in front of the boarding house. He simply appeared, as if out of nowhere, the same way he would disappear five years later. He seems to have been a handsome man, six-foot-three and slim as a whip, with big arms, greased black hair, and gray eyes like a wolf's. His face was long and angular, with a rugged jaw, a large nose, and a clefted chin like Kirk Douglas's. The day that Jim first saw my mother, he'd shown up at the boarding house in overalls and work boots; the landlady knew nothing about the drifter except that he was good with a wrench, polite to her boarders, and not unexciting to look at.

It was a sweltering afternoon, Marcia said. My mother was rubbing suntan oil on her legs and shoulders, the straps of her sundress pushed down. The girls were both in new bathing suits and jumping over the sprinklers when the tall stranger loped across the lawn swinging his toolbox. He smiled at my mother and she smiled back; a few minutes later, she wandered inside as the girls watched. According to Marcia, she found my father on his back underneath the upstairs sink, knocking a hammer against a pipe, and offered to get him a Coke. I can only assume what happened next, knowing my mother and her allure. When she handed my father the bottle of Coke, he must have been careful to touch her fingers and, when she turned around to leave, asked her to keep him company. I can see Ida sitting on the john and watching him work, my father sneaking unashamed looks at her chest, and noticing her melon-brushed lips—the same orange color she's always worn—like the inside of a ripe cantaloupe. When my father gently kicked the door shut and pulled my mother down on the floor, I'm sure that she made no effort to stop him.

· nine ·

Try to imagine your own conception. Conjure the primal scene in your mind, your parents' bodies thrashing together, your mother's hands—the hands that served dinner, held yours at the crosswalk, dabbed your forehead with Vicks in the winter—clutching at your father's hips as he heaves and grinds and moans above her. Imagine being shot into life as their bodies finally convulse together, the homunculus, the nub of you, snaking its way through utter darkness till it punctures the stupendous ovum. Imagine your parents lying there afterwards, your father's face flushed as he watches your mother, wondering where she retreated to so often, the woman-place where he can't find her. Does she already know that you've entered her life, or has she drifted somewhere else? Have you ever wondered what she was thinking at the moment you first took root inside her, and whether your mother's hazy thoughts might have been your first musings too? Whether her mood, and your father's as well, the smell of the room, the measure of light, their histories, hopes, and true intentions, the wealth or lack of love between them, the dreams they shared or would never share, might have affected the seed being planted, and the shape of what you became? How can we know when memory begins? Can we be sure we're not already present at the moment of our conception—not physically, of course, but in retrospect, through alchemy and imagination, the stories we're told about how we were made and who the people were who made us?

I was conceived on a bathroom floor by a woman trying to forget herself and a man who materialized out of nowhere, according to what I've been told. After her divorce from Milty became final, Ida married the fix-it man and moved with the girls to a small apartment in the San Fernando Valley, not far from Aunt Ruth's. With both daughters gone, Grandma and Grandpa sold the store in the Bronx and followed my mother and Ruth to the Valley. Though Grandpa was violently opposed to Ida's marrying a gentile—let alone a *shagitz* without a job—my father's willingness to convert (and receive Avraham as his Jewish name) persuaded Grandpa to give his blessing, along with a nominal dowry. There does not seem to have been much courtship; it's never been clear to me why they married except that both needed someone to hold. My mother didn't love him, exactly; rather, she seems to have craved his body. Once, when she'd been drinking too much, and I was in the throes of my own pubescent confession, Ida admitted to me that she'd never seen *that much man* in her entire life. Their sexual connection seems to have been so profound that the lack of loftier feelings could be overlooked. From what I can gather, they rolled along on this erotic wave for a couple of years before they capsized. Ruth's husband, Marty, helped Jim get hired at the garage of the trucking company where he worked, and where my mother soon took a job in the office, leaving the girls with Yetta, the oversized widow who lived next door. My mother was popular with the truckers but careful not to lead them on or do anything else to make my father jealous. She was tired of trouble, Jim seemed to love her, the girls worshipped him, and she was pregnant again. At twenty-nine, she wanted some peace from the turmoil she'd been stirring up since womanhood came to her prematurely.

The only man Mom ever loved walked into her life at this very juncture, catching her completely off-guard. Shapeless and nerdy, with a wavy hairline too low on his forehead, freckled arms, and pants that bagged around his rear, Julie held no attraction at all for her his first morning on the job, when he came into the dispatch office to pour himself a cup of coffee. He was rendered even less attractive by being such a gentleman, and when Julie struck up a friendly conversation, my mother felt no threat to the vows she was determined to keep. She seems to have enjoyed his politeness; masculine attention of Julie's restrained kind came as a welcome novelty and put her at ease. He didn't leer at her body or make innuendoes as he spoke. Leaving the office that first day, Julie shook her hand and told her how glad he was to have made her acquaintance.

These easy conversations continued whenever they were alone in the office. They marveled over California and how *back east* seemed like prison now, compared to the mountains and palm trees and sea. While my father was out back fixing transmissions, black-armed in his overalls, and Uncle Marty was out on the road, these morning talks became more frequent. Julie had free time on his hands, and over the next few weeks he told Ida about his lonely home life with a sickly wife and daughters who didn't seem to like him. My mother must have admitted to Julie that her daughters did not seem to like her either, and that sometimes the feeling was mutual. (These confessions provoked some laughter, especially being told to a stranger.) Julie admitted that he wanted a son but that his wife could bear no more children; my mother was hoping for a boy, too, though till then Julie hadn't realized that she was pregnant. He must have been gracious in that moment, telling Ida her husband was one lucky man, but my mother would have rolled her eyes and assured this naïve man that she was no picnic. I imagine him touching her hand just then—whatever he did made a chink in her armor. His gentleness, their innocent talk, the fact that Julie appeared to want nothing more than her company over coffee and doughnuts, softened a spot for him to get through.

"I never knew what hit me," she said, describing those first conversations to me. "I'd never met a man like that. Before I knew it, it was too late."

I knew that my mother was telling the truth. Even as a very young boy, I could feel her change when she said Julie's name. The hardness in her face went away. "He's the only man I've ever loved," she'd tell me when we were alone sometimes in the early morning while she drank her tea, while she waited for the one night a week that Julie came to see her during the fourteen years that she was his mistress. I enjoyed these moments of closeness with her, the unusual softness of her smile, too much to feel betrayed. I wanted so much for her to be happy, to see her eyes grow warm this way, that I didn't care what her happiness cost us. I didn't realize till many years later how this very happiness—and the havoc it would cause—helped to chase my father away and changed the course of all that came later.

· ten ·

I've never met anyone like Sullivan before. He's straight out of central casting, a private eye with a capital P. He's attacking this job like a hunter, sniffing along this trail and that, one finger up in the air to tell which way the wind is blowing, beating bushes, flushing the trees with the single-minded certainty that he will find his prey. His assurance seems unflagging, and after a few weeks he begins to convince me that we may actually find our man.

In the meantime, his style keeps me entertained. Along with the memos flooding my mailbox come cryptic notes, some of them so film noir they make me laugh. I read them out loud to Louis. "We will reach him on a *ruse*," I report like Edward G. Robinson, when Sullivan reports a promising lead in California. Or, "On March 9, Investigator D.B. proceeded to the New York Public Library Annex for old phone books." I imagine one of Sul-

livan's assistants slithering down Fifth Avenue in a trenchcoat,
white pages strapped against his body.

It all seems very camp.

Then I remember that this isn't a game and my stomach gets
tight and I ask myself—again—what I'll actually do if he tracks
my father down. Hearing Sullivan's bluff assurance of *promising
leads* and *possible suspects* is making success seem uncomfortably
close. There's been another weird shifting as well: I've started to
smell my father's ghost. Just this morning while I was shaving, the
citrus scent of the canned foam evoked his ghost in three dimensions and brought back an episode I had forgotten. My father had
been seated on the bathroom sink when the basin had ripped
away from the wall and hot water spewed from an open pipe.
There'd been pandemonium suddenly, pots and pans and steam
and screaming. He'd lifted me fast before I got scalded; I must
have been sitting there watching him shave, which I often did when
we'd finished showering. He'd wrap me up in a big striped towel
and sit me down on the toilet to observe his morning ritual. I'd
gaze up at the bottom of his chin as he ran his razor through the
whiteness. I could see his ribs, I think, and the shape of his penis
under the towel. His face was too high to see from my perch. All
I saw was a square jutting chin, a horsehair brush being twirled in
a soap dish, the silver razor blade slicing through bubbles. Remembering these moments this morning, I could almost feel his
presence beside me at the sink, the heaviness of him over my
shoulder. It's as if I've begun to conjure him, as if by allowing him
back as a prospect, making way for the notion of his return, a re-
entry process has already started. As this spectral contract is made,
something equally eerie occurs: each time I become aware of this

ghost, a voice inside me responds to its closeness, trying to meet it before it dissolves. This responding voice is indistinct, barely a tingle in my throat. Yet each time this happens I'm left with the sense of a dialogue starting between this presence and some inchoate part of myself, muffled beyond hearing.

· eleven ·

My mother cried when I was born, but perhaps it had nothing to do with joy, or with trying to save her marriage. Perhaps she wept because she loved Julie, and wished that I had been his son.

She kept her love affair secret at first, and until the time I was two or three, we seem to have been a happyish family. My father was popular with Marcia and Joyce, who rarely ever heard from Milty, while I was a precocious brat who demanded incessant attention. Every night at five-thirty when my father pulled into the driveway, I'd make a flying leap at him, according to Marcia, he'd lift me high up over his head, and I'd spread my arms out like airplane wings. I don't remember this at all but it fits the picture I've been given, of a blue-collar guy training his son to be the rough-and-tumble boy that American dads wanted back in the Fifties. He'd let me ride shotgun in his pickup, my hair greased back like his into a shiny pompadour; on weekend picnics in the park, Mom and the girls watched from a blanket as he taught me how to catch a ball. There were barbecues in the backyard, my mother's hair held above the ear with a Kon Tiki clip like Loretta Young's. Marcia and Joyce wore bobby socks, we watched the Sullivan show on Sundays, rabbit ears tuning the TV set. My mother made friends in the neighborhood—big-haired Rita, who dressed like a hooker, and great big Yetta the widow, three hundred pounds in a flowered muumuu, brick-red hair straight out of a bottle, cat's-eye glasses on a pearly chair, and a heart as big as Latvia. Every Sunday night, my mother played calookie at Yetta's and left Marcia in charge of the house. My father went off in his truck by himself. Joyce made Sloppy Joes from a can. I sneaked my mother's orange jellies from the lazy susan, and stayed up till she came home smelling of vodka and cigarettes and the Jean Naté powder she fluffed in her armpits.

This happiness was a sham, of course; a masquerade of suburban bliss. Not only was she in love with Julie, seeing him every chance she could, but my father's persona had begun to crack, revealing dark qualities that no one had suspected. Shortly after Belle was born, he was fired from the trucking company for reasons my mother could never uncover. This led to a spate of chronic lying and the fabrication of complex stories, one lie snowballing into another till Jim had forgotten what the truth was. He found odd jobs that didn't last (or pay) for reasons that seemed far-fetched. Either the boss had broken a hand, or forgotten to sign the paychecks, or gone bankrupt, or locked out the workers. My mother caught him again and again in these dog-ate-my-homework tales till she scarcely believed a word from his mouth. His lying was pathological, she said, and the more grandiose my father's lies grew, the farther he slipped into make-believe. He borrowed money from Grandpa to start his own repair shop, then claimed the garage had gone up in flames that destroyed not only the rental equipment but Grandpa's money and the business license as well. My mother defended him as long as she could, reasoning, I suppose, that at least *her* lies didn't threaten our survival. But soon their conflicts turned scary and vicious. Marcia would take us into the bedroom and cover Belle's ears with her hands while my parents battled. I was told that these rampages lasted for months and that one night my father stormed out of the house and didn't come back. My mother had the locks changed, and everyone thought that he was gone for good till the night he came back to kidnap me.

I wish that I could pause here and tell you about the sadness I felt after he left—the nights I spent waiting, face to the window, for his truck to appear; the longing I felt for his male presence; nights spent sobbing into my pillow—but I don't remember this happening and neither do my sisters. I was four years old, ditched in a house full of difficult women, inquisitive beyond my years—yet I have no recollection at all of how I felt when he disappeared. It's almost as if the boy who loved him disappeared that night as well.

Instead, I remember poverty. After he left, we were destitute, and my mother, who stopped working when Belle was born, applied for welfare. We moved to an even smaller apartment where she scrambled every month to make the ninety-five-dollar rent. Sometimes we had nothing for dinner but noodles and Kool-Aid; sometimes Willy the butcher threw in an extra pound of hamburger meat when we went to his shop. My mother and Willy had a flirtation—he winked at her over the skirt steak and lamb chops. Willy used to pick me up and slide pieces of warm corned beef into my mouth.

"You like that, kid?"

"Thanks, Willy."

"You want some kishka?"

"Yum," I'd say, and he'd slip me a wedge of stuffed derma. "You eat good, you grow good," Willy would say, and then he'd dig his big hairy hands into my ribs and make me squirm. "What is this, skinny? Like a girl. Ain't you feeding him, Ida?"

"I'm feeding him."

"Well, you gotta feed him more!" And a couple of extra deli packages would find their way into the shopping basket.

Though I don't remember missing my father, I well recall the stigma of being the only kid at school who came from a broken home. That's what my kindergarten teacher called divorced families, *broken,* and the label stuck deep in my five-year-old mind. Being *underprivileged* on top of it put our family beyond the pale: this is the term my teacher used to explain to the class why I used a pink stub, instead of two quarters, to pay for my lunch at the cafeteria. The shame of this double humiliation forced me to lead separate lives throughout childhood—the one *out there* and the one *in here.* I refused to let school friends come to my house, and on parent days I lied to the teacher about why my mother was always absent (I didn't tell Mom there *were* parent days). I'd sit on the kitchen sink after school, watching the boys play basketball in the street; outside the window, they'd dribble and shoot and skin their knees in a world that seemed different from where we lived—

a bright, happy, open place like the TV world of laugh tracks and jingles captured behind the curved glass screen. I watched them as if from somewhere off-camera, from the bastard zone where nobody was looking.

Little Israel. That's what they called the sprawl of freshly planted suburbs along the brand new Hollywood Freeway where we lived. The neighborhood was almost completely Jewish, with ranch houses and swimming pools, and motorboats parked in driveways. Dads came home in jackets and ties; Moms wore pastel-colored capris and packed rugelach in their kids' lunchboxes. At the end of one of these middle-class blocks, our crumbly old apartment building sat like a transient motel, full of lunatics, pensioners, immigrants, and losers. Next door to our three cramped rooms lived an ancient hag named Mrs. Sims, who spent most of her time behind boarded-up windows, spitting at anyone who crossed her path on the rare occasions she came outside. One early evening out back by the trash cans, eyes popping out from beneath her babushka, Mrs. Sims swung a length of chain at my mother, two gnarled fingers held out like a pitchfork, and put a Slavic curse on her. Sometime later, we watched two men in white clothes pull Mrs. Sims out of the apartment, dragging her crusty heels across the pavement, into a waiting truck. A gang of ugly, bull-necked Samoans slept four to a room in the apartment upstairs and roasted whole pigs on a spit on the back lawn for their monthly *luau*. Next to them was a family of rat-faced hillbillies whose oldest girl taught me to play strip poker so she could show me her red pubic hair. Her name was Rima Louise. She liked to call me a white-trash Jew.

Grandpa refused to help us; Ida had made this bed, he thought, and we kids would just have to lie in it. After men from Sears and Roebuck appeared one day to repossess our living room set, we brought furniture home from the Salvation Army, big, ugly plaid stuff that gave us a rash when we sat on it. Utilities were touch-and-go: one month we'd be without a phone; the following month the lights would go out, leaving us to eat Chef Boyardee by the light of *yahrzeit* candles. Once in a while Julie would help us, but my mother hated to ask him for money. "I cried because I had no shoes till I saw the man who had no feet," she'd say when I wanted something new, as if I cared about some footless stranger. I wanted a Schwinn Sting Ray and Beatle-boots, not a lesson in charity. The tug-of-war between my mother's few dollars and what four children needed in order to feel normal became the background noise of our home, my mother screaming and wringing her hands, we kids simply wanting what other kids had.

"When can I just think about me?" she'd plead sometimes, overwhelmed by our relentless needs. This question consistently enraged me. I hated my mother's monotonous *no* and the second-class feeling infecting our family. I hated her obsession with Julie, the selfishness crowding us out of her heart. I hated hearing her beg him for attention, watching her hold her breath for Tuesdays, the way she ran to his car when he honked, teetering on her high heels, clutching her little straw valise, kissing him in the front seat while we watched from behind the screen door. I hated her stumbling in the next morning, tousled and gloomy, and telling me—when she looked up from the kitchen table to where I was standing—that I was the only man who'd never leave her. My mother would hold out her arms and I'd go, only half-willingly, knowing that her hug would crush me and I'd have to fight from crying too when I felt her tears against my skin. "You're my Rock of Gibraltar," she'd say, resting her cheek on my belly, as if I were something solid and big instead of a skinny boy in pajamas wanting my breakfast, too scared to move. I stood there while she hugged me and cried, wondering what rock she was talking about and seemed to need so desperately. I wondered if this rock was in me somewhere and how could I find it in time to save her. When my mother stopped crying and pulled away, she'd leave me smeared with orange lipstick.

Her grief got worse as the years went by, and in time I would grow to pity her. Though I didn't have words to explain what I knew, I realized that something was broken in Ida—that *she* was the broken thing in our home—and wished that I could fix her somehow. I knew as a boy, without being told, that she was on the verge of destruction, but when I asked her why she was so sad and didn't bother getting dressed, why she lay in the bathtub for hours, muttering and knocking her head, dropping cigarettes into the toilet—I could hear them under the door go *psss*, then my mother whispering *I want to die*—she pushed me away more often than not and told me to worry about myself. The prospect of losing her panicked me, and though she was sinking I couldn't stop her. Pity and panic—my childhood companions—and burning around them a terrible rage because I couldn't change how things were at home. In my angriest, most powerless moments, I wished for a man to walk in the door and put the situation right; to save my mother—save all of us—from going under and not coming up. I couldn't do it all by myself.

· twelve ·

A few weeks after calling Mac Sullivan, I'm standing barefoot on a cold linoleum floor as Doctor G checks my naked body inch by inch for signs of trouble. He runs his fingers along my groin, behind my ears, under my jawline and arms. He taps the four quadrants of my back, asks me to breathe deep, listens to my chest with a stethoscope. He shines a flashlight into my mouth, inspects around the tongue a long time, then shoots the light straight into my eyes. His breath is prehistoric. When he sits on a stool to check my feet, I cup my privates and watch him separate my toes, then palpate the strawberry birthmark on my leg. He asks me to bend over the table and uses a rubber glove to feel inside, for bumps and lumps without a word of bedside humor. Finally the exam is over.

"You're a very lucky man," he says. I've never met Doctor G before. When I first sat down in his office to give him my medical history, he was mortified to hear that I hadn't had an exam in three years. He informed me—as if this were news—that this disease could be very sneaky. I told him that I was aware of that but that I've never felt healthier. What I didn't admit was that staying as far from doctors as possible had been, for the last decade, an integral part of my plan for survival. I resisted the urge to ask Doctor G why on earth I'd put trust in an M.D. when science couldn't help me get better; nor do I admit to him that I'm not here completely by choice. A friend has shamed me into making the appointment, implying that I've been cowardly. I was petrified walking into this office; I'm petrified now as Doctor G drains five vials of blood from my arm, afraid of what the lab will discover. Truth serum, I think, as the vials fill up. My concerned friend called it information. "Get the information," he'd said, "it's better to know than not to know." Information! I'd wanted to protest, as if there were nothing alarming at stake, as if we were probing a neutral subject. But my friend would not have understood. The gun isn't currently aimed at his head, and when you feel safe you can't understand.

"No visible symptoms," the doctor concludes, once I'm dressed and ready to leave. Then he attempts a smile but is far too depressed to carry it off. Doctor G has an undertaker's face: doleful eyes, grim lips, no vitality whatsoever.

"Appearances can be deceptive," I say as a preemptive strike, or perhaps to sound brave, I'm not sure which. Confirming my worst fears, Doctor G agrees with me.

· thirteen ·

Every time the phone rings I jump. I'm screening my calls in case of bad news. Sullivan checks in, unfailingly cheerful, telling me to keep the faith. Joe calls, wanting an update. Belle calls, wanting an update. Barbara calls, as she does every morning, and hers is the only call I pick up.

"You sound terrible," she tells me.

All I've said is hello, but that's all it takes for us to tune in. Barbara is my surrogate sister; we know each other like blood relatives. I remind her that I've hardly slept in the two days since my doctor appointment, and that when I do manage to drift off a little, I'm woken up by scary dreams. Last night, I was crawling down the fire escape with my mother when a skinny man with a half a face came leaping over my building and landed on the aluminum roof. I woke up in a cold sweat. Looking out the window now, I see the black boot in the roof's corner. Barbara tells me, *once again*, that I could use some therapy. I thank her for this brilliant news flash and make an excuse about needing to work.

I can't work, however, and haven't been able to think straight for weeks. According to Barbara, this is auspicious; it means that I'm on the verge of a breakthrough. She's been telling me since this search began that more was at stake here than I will admit; that what seemed to begin on a whim was, in fact, a life-changing decision. Before I hired Mac Sullivan, I'd consulted Barbara to see what she thought. We were sitting in her living room on the Upper East Side; Barbara was in sweatpants on the couch, surrounded by pages of her novel-in-progress, called *Looking for Love in All the Wrong Places*. Longing in its many forms—romantic, artistic, political, holy—has been Barbara's pet theme for twenty years, in plays, articles, and now this book. She's convinced that longing dominates the world—not mere *desire*, she hastens to say, but a kind of aching, yearning hunger for some unreachable person or thing that will finally, magically, make us feel whole and ease our sense of emptiness. Our lives are determined, Barbara believes, by how we attempt to fill this emptiness, which illusion we attempt to seize on in hopes of filling up this hole. In the end, of course, the void can't be filled—as a practicing Buddhist, Barbara knows that. Still the pathos of longing fascinates her and keeps her touchingly, visibly, fractured; after Louis, she's the most nakedly vulnerable person I know.

"You've got to do this," she'd said. "It's long overdue."

"I don't see why."

Barbara lowered her glasses on her nose—she likes to look

librarianesque to stress a point—and blinked her green eyes. "Wake up."

"One good reason."

She held out her arms in a gesture she favors, like a child imploring the sky.

"That's you, not me."

"That's everyone."

"I don't need a father."

"Everyone needs a father," said Barbara. "Not the flesh-and-blood kind necessarily. But what the father—the *Father*—stands for."

"It doesn't stand for anything."

"And you don't think that's a tiny problem?"

"You really don't miss what you've never had."

And round and round we went. Barbara insisted that it was the search, not the conclusion, that mattered, and that it was a part of myself I was seeking. She'd told me to think symbolically, and frame this pursuit in terms of self-knowledge, feeling authentic—grown up—as a man. Authentic indecision is all I felt when I'd left her apartment.

Louis added to the confusion. We'd been living together for only three months, and hardly a day of it had passed without some kind of domestic drama. Cramped living was part of the problem, but more than that was the wrenching I felt between fear of entrapment and wanting a partner. My inner war left him sad and confused and caused enormous friction between us. I hated myself for feeling so split, ashamed of my neuroses and embarrassed by Louis's unflagging patience. The struggle to keep our fragile peace had left him exhausted; a father hunt, and the potential for more upheaval, did not sound appealing.

"Maybe Barbara's right," I'd said.

"Barbara doesn't live with us," Louis had answered. We were sitting outside on the stoop, smoking. Louis was wearing a baseball cap turned backward on his head. "She's speaking in generalizations."

When Louis was eight, his father ran away with his secretary, leaving Louis alone with his mother. He'd spent his boyhood the same way I had, trying to fill his father's big shoes and ease the pain of his mother's wounds. Where Ida was cool and distant, Louis's mother was all-consuming; he nursed her complaints and cleaned up her grief like a sucker fish working the bottom of a bowl. When she couldn't sleep, Louis would spend the night in her bed. "It's us against the world," his mother would say when Louis waited on alternate weekends for the car his father sent to the suburbs to bring him into Manhattan. He dreaded leaving his mother alone and felt like a traitor when he was in his father's house.

Now, on the stoop, he had turned extra quiet. We watched the bridge-and-tunnel kids—boys in elephantine pants with gang tattoos around skinny arms—sprawled on other people's car hoods, drinking beer from cans in brown paper bags, groping girls in push-up bras and lacquered hair, dancing to the radio. "What's going on?" I asked.

"You got me thinking about my father."

A hefty girl in a black lace blouse was tongue-kissing a kid who looked no more than fourteen; another girl sucked on her boyfriend's finger.

"He hurt me," said Louis.

"He hit you?" I asked.

"Worse," he answered. "At least to me."

"What happened?"

"It's stupid."

"Just tell me," I said.

Louis stubbed out his cigarette. "I had this record, an old 45," he said. "There was a sad song on one side and a happy song on the other. I'd lock myself in the bedroom and play that sad song over and over till it drove my father nuts. He banged on the door and told me to quit it, but I didn't care. That song was how I felt inside—I wanted him to hear it. 'What kind of kid listens to that crap?' he'd say."

I pictured Louis at seven years old, not knowing what to say to his father, repeating that sad song alone in a room.

"He wanted me to cheer up but I couldn't. Finally, he just grabbed the record and cracked it over his knee." Louis shrugged and shook his head. "That was it—it was over for me."

"What was over?"

"The love," said Louis. "At least the connection. I hardly saw him again till he died. In the hospital, he said that he loved me. I guess I forgave him. I'm not really sure. I just know it's better to walk away sometimes."

"You're saying that to me?" I'd asked.

"I don't know what I'm saying," he'd said.

Shortly afterward, I made a date with Samuel. Samuel and I have been friends for years, though we don't see each other often. It's a friendship composed of peaks and valleys: every few months we get together for one of our marathon catch-up sessions and talk passionately, for hours, about surprisingly personal things. Our lives have run similar paths through the years, as seekers, skeptics, conflicted lovers, and this time we found ourselves, once again, in overlapping territory. Samuel had just returned from several months in Israel, where he had sat at his father's deathbed. I was anxious to hear all about it.

"Being with him at the end changed my life completely," he said. We'd chosen a table near the front of our favorite cafe. Samuel's shaven head was silhouetted against the window, dark eyes squinting through the smoke of an Indian cigarette he held like a joint between his fingers. "Without question the best thing I ever did. I still can't believe it turned out this way."

I egged him on. I needed to hear this.

"My father and I had never been close. My mother used to tell me when I was a kid that he wasn't fit to be a parent. She may have been right, but how could I tell—she always kept a wall between him and me, so he and I were distant strangers. He lived with us, but always apart, like the shell of a father." Samuel shook his head in amazement. "Then he got sick, and for some weird reason I was the one he wanted close by. I saw how tender the man really was. Sitting those weeks with him saved my life."

I felt a sudden pang of envy, remembering my mother's refrain about what a bad father Jim would have been—how I wasn't the son he'd wanted and what a troubled man he'd been. I'd feel hurt sometimes when she said it, as if it were me she was cutting down.

"I'd been in big trouble for so long," said Samuel. Sometime around his fortieth birthday, Samuel's life had seemed to cave in around him. After twenty years of self-inquiry, this crisis had come as if out of nowhere, leaving him unable to cope. Having thought about suicide, he'd checked himself into a hospital and fallen out of touch with me for two years. Now he filled me in on what had happened. "My whole sense of meaning had gone. Nothing mattered to me anymore. I felt so lost and sad. Then a doctor explained to me what was really going on."

"What was it?" I asked, sounding more urgent than I intended.

"It's hard to explain," said Samuel, pausing to gather his thoughts. "But I realized how much of me was missing as a man. I'd been trying so hard not to be like my father, the image of him that I'd made up, that I had no idea who I really was. I had all this power but no foundation, this huge abyss was underneath where my father's strength should have been, the memory of him, his belief in me. That's why my life never quite came together. When I got out of the hospital, I was raging. Then he got sick and called for me, and all of that began to change."

I was stirred by this story, fully aware that Samuel was describing us both. He lit another smoke and grinned. "We like to pretend we're all grown up, *handling it*. What a joke! Sitting with my father, I felt like I was five years old. I was amazed to see how much I still craved his approval after all these years, though I believed that I didn't care. I *still* wanted him to be proud of me. He loved to be pampered, just like me—I just sat there next to the bed and touched him. One day, my mother asked me to shave him and when I finished, he kissed my hand. He was too sick to talk, but he looked at me and smiled with my mother and older brother watching.

"Something happened when he kissed my hand—how can I say it? My father lived through his hands. He was a baker, and in his spare time he liked to garden. His hands were his soul."

"Like you," I said. Samuel does healing touch for a living.

"It was as if I was accepting the part of my father that's in me. I know my father felt it, too, because he trusted me by then. The sicker he grew, the more he depended. Anything to do with his body, he asked for me to help him. I changed his catheter every morning—the first time I did it, I was actually shaking. Touching him there was extremely strange, so *intimate*. It reminded me of the story in the Bible when Isaac dies. The blessing was meant to go to the older son, and whoever got the blessing would thrive. Jacob was younger than Esau, the way I was younger than my brother, but he managed to touch his father's thigh. Touching the father's thigh was the symbol of being blessed. I knew when my father was dying that he was blessing me."

Samuel stopped talking for a minute. "That simple touch was more important than anything I'd been through before," he said. "All the teachers, the books, the achievements. No words. Just that." He reached under the table and touched my leg with his finger. "Just that."

When Samuel left, I stayed behind, writing this story down in my journal. I thought about what it means to be blessed when speaking of a father and son, and realized why finding my own father had never inspired me whatsoever. It wasn't his physical presence I longed for, as Barbara had already suggested; I didn't care about genealogy or connecting with him in a soap-opera way. But when I thought about having his blessing, something began to crystallize: I felt in my bones, for the first time, how much I longed for his spiritual touch, for him to tell me that I was worthy. I'd felt fundamentally *unblessed*, as a person and as a man; that was the core of the grief I'd carried as well as the key to why I would hire Mac Sullivan. Some time later, I came across a passage from Kafka's letter to his father that captured this pain precisely. "My writing was about you," he wrote. "In it I only poured out the grief I could not sigh at your breast." Grief, I thought, but also questions—fear, confusion, achievement, nostalgia—and joy in being alive at all.

· fourteen ·

If men were a foreign country after my father left, then naked men were its jungle interior, full of primitive, frightening forces, fierce and carnivorous. Between the ages of seven and twelve, this territory mesmerized me—in an anthropological way—for being so alien and taboo. Female bodies were less intriguing; they were everywhere I turned, in all their cloven intimacy. Our home was like a child's circus of bouncing breasts and hairless buttocks, robes parted sloppily over breakfast, brown nipples, pink nipples, underarm nubs. There were narrow shoulders, jiggling triceps, high-arched feet, and punctured lobes, eyelids scrubbed red with cold cream (pentimento of liner and shadow), hairspray fumes and douches and powders, menstrual accouterments, and underthings hanging from knob and nozzle—girdles and panties, brassieres and hose: the packing and wrappers of female flesh. Such was the decor of my boyhood, so overwhelming it seemed sometimes that the house itself was a female body, a great surrounding egg, with me the lone sperm swimming around it, getting caught, breaking loose, tiny next to the egg's massive girth. Women's bodies were as common to me as men's must be to boys with fathers, tensionless, de-sexed, and familiar.

When now and then I happened upon naked men, however, I was awestruck by their strangeness.

Most summer afternoons when I was eight, Mom would drop me off at the public pool to get me out of her hair.

"Get a move on!" she'd shout at me from the T-bird in the driveway. I'd be rushing around the apartment, packing her little straw valise with my standard gear: swimming trunks, combo lock, towel, two mayonnaise-on-white bread sandwiches, a bottle of RC Cola, and a scribble pad. I'd be racking my brain over which of my two favorite books to bring, *The Biography of Madame Curie* or *The Adventures and Discoveries of Marco Polo*. Madame Curie would win out most often, though I'd read the paperback five times already and now only skimmed for the heroic parts, such as when Marie keeps on looking for radium even though she knows she has cancer. Reading this part always made me cry. I was devoted to Madame Curie; she was the kind of great human being I wanted to be when I grew up, except that she was a woman. At eight, that seemed like a bridgeable gap.

On that particular day, when Mom left me at the curb by the park, I hid the valise inside the towel and carried it under my arm the way boys did with their books at school, rather than swing it by the handle like a girl with a purse. Approaching the changing room, I felt my stomach begin to cramp. The changing room was my personal hell, the only place on earth where I was forced to undress in public, and was guaranteed to see naked men. I'd pause in front of the bungalow between the doors for women and men, then slip like a trespasser to the right.

The room was cool and full of puddles, fairly empty, smelling of chlorine, b. o., Old Spice—like Grandpa wore—and the powder I'd seen men slop between their legs to keep themselves dry. An old man with chicken legs and blue skin shuffled around in rubber sandals, a black father slipped his little boy's arms through the sleeves of a green Giants T-shirt. A man sang in a low voice from the direction of the showers. I went to the locker I always used, at the far end of the last row and out of sight of the door, put my valise down, quickly dropped my shorts and pulled on my bathing suit, keeping my shirt on. I didn't like people to see my chest; I felt shy of it the way girls did. I knew this was wrong and that other boys didn't care, but I was still self-conscious.

"You're *strange*," Mom would often say when I came out of the bathroom with a towel wrapped under my armpits like Marcia and Joyce.

"Not as strange as you," I'd reply.

I rolled up my socks and put them in my sneakers in the locker, then folded my shorts and placed them neatly on top. I removed the sandwich, notepad, and books, then rolled them together into the towel. Just as I was putting the valise into the locker, the guy from the shower came around the corner and stood right next to me with his towel wrapped around his butt.

"Hey," he said, rubbing up his hair.

I didn't look directly at him. "Hey," I said under my breath. I tried to shove the valise into the locker, sideways first, then longways. I got flustered when it wouldn't fit.

"Give you a hand with that?"

"I got it," I said, forcing the suitcase in and ripping the handle off in the process. Out of the corner of my eye, I could see that the guy had black hair on his toes, just like my father had. The sight was gross but interesting.

"It never fails," he said, leaning over me to turn the combo on his lock. "My locker's right on top of yours." I froze in fear of knocking against his arm as he pulled out a pair of briefs. He dropped the towel on the floor as a mat and then stepped into his underwear. I did everything I could not to ogle his body.

"Good book?" he asked me. On the cover of the paperback was a bad pencil drawing of a woman in a high-necked dress, bent over a microscope.

"She discovered radium," I said.

"Really?" He pounded a bottle of golden oil and smoothed some onto his hair. He was Latin-looking and very handsome, a man's man, like Willy at the butcher shop, the kind of man Mom liked. All the girls must like him, I thought. "Radium," he said, wiping his greasy hands on the towel. "That's a big deal."

"It makes X rays."

"That's right." The guy was standing in front of the mirror in his white underpants and bright white T-shirt, parting his hair in front of the mirror. "We need X rays, that's for sure."

He wasn't making fun of me. In fact, he seemed to be really nice, and instead of hurrying out, I fiddled with trying to stick my pencil through the spiral binding of my notebook while he fixed his hair in front of the mirror. He looked both ways to check out his comb job, slapped some Aqua Velva on his cheeks, curled back his lips to inspect his teeth, and came back to his locker. He took a short-sleeved checked shirt from where it was hanging and held it up in front of him like a matador with a cape. When I looked up, I could see straight up the loose white sleeve of his T-shirt into his hairy armpit.

I sat there staring up his shirtsleeve as if I'd been struck by a primeval vision. Time seemed to stop as I gazed upward—frozen—struck by the animal fact of his maleness, what men had hidden in their secret places, what I'd have someday but had never quite been aware of before. I gazed into his underarm hair as if into a wilderness, and can still feel the shudder that I felt then, knowing that I was seeing my future, and that a furry beast was inside me, too, waiting to bust through my smooth skin and turn me into something else. Though I vaguely recalled my father's body towering over me in the shower, my memories had so constellated around his penis, swinging at eye level, that the rest of him had been eclipsed. I could hardly associate that slab of gristle with the acorn between my legs; now, however, I saw the connection.

Sitting there, awestruck and scared, I wondered what this man's body knew, what secrets were hidden where I couldn't see them—what secrets were hidden inside me as well. Long after he'd left with a hearty so-long, I lingered where I was on the bench, floating between his world and the androgynous one that I knew.

· fifteen ·

Doctor G has bad news. "We need to talk right away," he says, voice tight around the edges as he speaks into my answering machine. *Need* is the giveaway. My feet go cold, then my calves, then the rest of my legs and my hands. I lose all feeling below my waist, the ground seems very far away. I sit on the couch and stop breathing. I tell myself that I'm overreacting. I force myself to take a breath, but the oxygen gets trapped in my throat.

When I call Doctor G an hour later, he tells me in a low, flat voice that my numbers are very bad. The cells that kill what's trying to kill me are one-tenth what they ought to be. He tells me that treatment is critical and must begin immediately. There's no statistical reason to hope that treatment will have any lasting effect, but Doctor G says that I must do something. He informs me in badly upholstered language that, numerically speaking, I've passed the point of no return. It's just a matter of time, he implies—using clinical terms that offer no comfort—before the bottom falls out completely. I've nursed enough friends to know what this looks like. I hang up the phone feeling ice-cold.

Instinctively, I go to the mirror. When I was a boy feeling lost and scared, I'd sit for hours alone in the bathroom, talking to my own reflection, asking questions and answering them myself, trying to get to the bottom of things, to find my way to solid ground. If I talked long enough, and made enough sense, I sometimes succeeded in feeling safe. Now, without thinking, I repeat these steps, holding onto the basin enamel, leaning my head toward the glass and staring into my eyes for something to buoy me, an anchor to steady me so I don't drown. I speak gently to myself, *calm down, easy now, relax, you're fine,* as a mother might do to a scared kid, but when this doesn't help I try addressing myself man to man. *Get a grip, steady now, you can fight, you're strong as a horse, nobody knows what's going to happen, keep your eye on the goddamn ball.* This man's voice hardly seems to be mine; I hear it in the distance somewhere, beyond a babble of cries and whimpers. The illusion of safety is crashing now, the voice of reason can't hold it together.

In the mirror, a dying man is staring at me, a sweat-covered corpse with open eyes. I sit on the toilet, drop my head, and count the squares on the bathroom floor. Eighty-eight slate gray, one-inch tiles from wall to door. My childhood tiles were gold and white—bigger than these, with lighter grout. My father's feet were white as well, enormous with long misshapen toes—five times the size of my feet when I placed them heel-to-heel against his. How many squares would his feet have covered—twenty at least, I estimate now. Then one by one, to steady my stomach, I count out twenty beside my own foot. My toes are just as ugly as his were, my ankles also bony and weak. He wrapped me in a towel that matched his and rubbed me hard when we finished showering, slapped Vitalis on his palms, and parted my hair with a dimestore comb. Then he said something, what was it?—I can't quite remember the words, but the tone was light and the words made him chuckle—something about the ladies, I think, and how they liked men who smelled good. My father smelled good—I can almost smell his lemon cologne now, the steam from our shower, the mint on my breath from the toothpaste we shared. I take a towel off the hook and bunch it into a ball in my lap. What would he say if he saw me now? What will I say if I see him again? This question suddenly sounds very different, urgent and real as Doctor G's voice. *We need to talk right away.* I cry for a minute then, sloppy and loud, get to my feet, wash my face, brush my teeth, and replace the towel. The sun is above the aluminum roof now. When the glare hits the mirror, my face disappears.

· sixteen ·

On the afternoon that my parents' marriage certificate finally arrives, I feel unexpectedly relieved. In all the weeks of waiting, through my mother's procrastination (which has felt a great deal like revenge), tired of making excuses every time Mac Sullivan calls to find out where the damned thing is, I haven't acknowledged my secret fear that maybe, just maybe, my parents hadn't been married at all.

Running upstairs with the envelope, I nearly flatten our downstairs neighbor, Marie.

"Jesus Christ, honey, watch out!" Marie is clutching the pilled pink neck of her ancient nightgown, ninety-year-old hands shaking, a tissue stuffed into one eyesocket (she only puts in the eye when she has to). In her prime, Marie was a stripper; now she sits in the apartment beneath ours blasting game shows and chain-smoking Kools, looking like a lizard in a negligee, a gash of red lipstick across her toothless mouth. She calls me down to screw in light bulbs and screams out the window *shut the hell up!* when Louis and I are fighting. She bangs her broom against the ceiling and meets us in the hall afterward, telling us to love each other, kissing us both on the cheeks.

"Where the hell you running to?" Marie asks now with a cycloptic blink.

"Important mail. Gotta go."

"You're not hurting that boy, are you?"

"Never," I say. "I just yell a lot."

"You hurt him and I'll kill you," says Marie, then teeters on stick-legs back into her cave.

Conspicuously, my mother has not included a note with the package. Both of us have been standoffish lately; we avoid each other when we're upset or have bad news we don't want to share. Several Sundays have come and gone without a phone call either way. I'm still reeling from Doctor G's call, and letting this search go forward, as if I've broken some contract with Ida that I never meant to sign. When I admit to Joe how guilty I feel, he tells me this is the cost of my livelihood. "Writers betray people for a living," he says. Naturally, this makes me feel worse. To stop the cold war from escalating, I call my mother the following Sunday.

Instantly, I know she's been drinking. It's ten A.M. on the west coast and before I can stop myself, I ask her why she's indulging so early.

"Mind your own damn business," she says.

"It is my business."

"No, it's not. Take care of yourself. I'll take care of me."

"I just asked."

"You're always asking."

"We hardly talk, Mom."

"That's not my fault."

"Nobody said it was," I say.

"Don't be sarcastic."

"I wasn't."

"Sarcastic mouth. Just like your father."

"What are you talking about?"

"Why do you always have to start trouble?"

"That isn't why I called," I say.

"You never know when to quit, do you? Can't leave well enough alone."

"Why are you so mad at me?"

"Who's mad?"

"Mom, please."

"My whole goddamn life I've been fighting."

"I know that," I say.

"I'm tired," she says.

"So let's not fight."

"Okay by me."

"Thanks for the thing you sent," I say.

"You're welcome."

"I really appreciate it."

"Bruce and I are watching a movie."

"I'll call you next Sunday."

"I won't hold my breath."

"I love you," I say.

"Like a hole in the head."

"I do."

My mother coughs. "I know."

"Okay?"

"Okay. I love you, too."

I hang up feeling angry and sad.

The marriage certificate surprises me in a number of ways. First, it reveals that my father, aged thirty on the first day of November, 1956, when Rabbi Emmanuel Katz performed the ceremony in Los Angeles, had already been divorced. Next, and most important for Sullivan, I learn his middle initial, J. Finally, the names of my paternal grandparents, James Matousek Sr. and the former Caroline Busch, both born in Illinois, are listed, adding phantom limbs to our scrawny, lop-sided family tree.

Useful as these details are, however, the most compelling revelation for me is my father's signature. I've never seen his writing before, and the sight of his name, written with his own hand, takes me by surprise. The lettering is delicate, almost florid, not the signature of a thug, an illiterate, or someone devoid of inner beauty. This photocopied signature, nearly four decades old, is the first tangible evidence of my flesh-and-blood father to turn up since he left, and may be the closest I ever come to having an actual fingerprint. It feels as rare and important to me as an artifact raised from the ocean floor.

When I take the certificate to Sullivan's office, he's out to lunch. His secretary takes it from me and slips it into the in-box with a note marked *very important*.

"Everything okay, honey?" asks Liz, smiling up at me from behind her desk, all crooked teeth and frosted lipstick, cavernous cleavage, and raccoon-tinted hair. Liz and I have become phone buddies.

"Fine," I say quickly.

"You sure?" she asks. "You look kind of thin."

"Nerves," I say. "Stressed out."

"So what's the scoop when you're stressed out and fat?" Liz stands up to show me her hips, which don't belong in a red leather skirt. "The hips that ate Manhattan," she laughs. "People get weird when they look for their parents."

"They must," I say. "It's a weird thing to do."

"I told Mac I'd pay him to lose mine." Liz uncaps a tin of Pringles and hands me a chip locked between inch-long talons. It tastes like paper sprayed with potato. "You really don't have to worry with Mac. He always finds who he's looking for. He really cares. Believe it or not, underneath the crapola, the guy's got a heart of gold."

"I believe it," I say.

Two weeks later, Sullivan sends me a narrowed-down list with the useful initial. There are only five James J's.

· seventeen ·

Poke . . . drip . . . doze . . . wait. I close my eyes and try to rest, but Doctor G's treatment room is a circus. There are five of us hooked up to IV poles. A Dominican queen is plumped up on cushions, yapping about his latest *papi* to a big-chested dancer girl in fuzzy leggings and an off-the-shoulder Madonna T-shirt. A Chelsea boy weightlifter is channel-surfing on the big-screen TV, flexing his calves in time to the remote. A skeletal man sleeps in an Eames chair, under an afghan, footrest up, Coke-bottle eyeglasses sliding down bumpy, clay-gray cheeks. Next to him, an old lady reads a romance novel, her bifocals hooked to a pearly chain. I imagine that she's his mother.

When I told my mother that I'd been infected, she said, "No child of mine will ever have to die alone." It was 1988—I was standing in a phone booth on a bison preserve in South Dakota, midway through a cross-country trip. I was speechless for a minute when she said this—I'd been putting off this call for months, dreading the panic I'd hear in her voice, finally calling on impulse—but Mom didn't sound panicked at all. She sounded stoical and brave. I couldn't understand this: she hadn't been brave when Marcia died; back then, she'd said that losing a child was the worst thing a parent could ever live through. And yet her response now gave me courage. "I'm fine," I told her. "Asymptomatic." Mom wasn't sure what that meant exactly. "I'll let you know if I ever need you." She never brought up the subject again.

At Doctor G's insistence, I've gone overnight from being someone who balked at taking an aspirin, to swallowing twenty toxic pills a day, having my blood drawn every four weeks, and sitting in this treatment room for ninety minutes, eight times a month, having prophylactic drips. One of the drugs makes my face hot—other than that, I'm impervious, though the other patients complain of side effects. The nurse, Evelyn, babies them shamelessly. She pours Gatorade into Styrofoam cups with our initials crayonned on on the side, and hands out homemade cookies she brings on the train from Ronkonkoma. The queen on the cushions squawks the most. Evelyn likes to call him Cupcake.

The Chelsea boy finds a movie he likes—*Invasion of the Body Snatchers*—and turns the volume up even higher. Evelyn turns her chair toward the set, and I double my drip-speed against her orders. There are two full bags on my pole left to empty—one yellow, one clear—and at this rate I'll be here for two hours. I close my eyes and try to find patience, think about a blue sky, think of the chimes on my fire escape, tinkle ding, tinkle ding, imagining each ring to be the echo of the enlightened mind, as the Tibetan who sold them to me described the sound. I repeat the mantra I

learned in India—*so hum, so hum*—I am peace, I am peace—
focusing on the Sanskrit syllables, one on the in-breath, one on the
out, to calm my mind in this miserable place while the pod people
shriek from the TV set. I time the mantra with my drip, *so hum,
so hum*, which feels today like water torture. I'd like to throttle the
boy with the muscles, kick the IV pole through the window.

So hum, I repeat in vain, over the din of these unserene
thoughts. Wherever I turn inwardly, I see trouble. Louis is taking
this very hard. I'm doing my best to appear optimistic, reminding
him that I'm not *really* sick, that nobody knows what the future
holds, but this forced bravado is lost on him. The day that Doctor
G called with my bad numbers, Louis began preparing to lose me.
After years of nursing Ronnie through his slow decline, years
spent following doctor's orders to feed Ronnie drugs that helped
to kill him, Louis's faith in medicine—indeed, his faith in rever-
sals of fortune—is kaput. He seems more depressed by the day, although he's struggling not to show it, and frightened for himself
as well.

So hum. The mantra is useless. The white-haired lady is click-
ing her dentures. I open my eyes and study her face—she's absorbed in her book, smiling lightly. Perhaps her heroine's being
ravished. When her son stirs under his blanket, she takes a tissue
out of her sleeve and dabs the sweat from the crease in his forehead. Her hands are large and spotted with age; she wears no wedding ring. My mother never wears her wedding ring, either. Her
hands are small and brown like a monkey's, with skinny fingers,
chewed-down nails, and wide, flat palms like mine. When we sat
alone in the kitchen together, me with my book, Ida with her
sand-colored tea and Pall Malls, I'd memorize her hands from

across the table so that today, thirty years later, I can still remember them down to the vein, better than the hands of any lover I've ever had, better than my own. I memorized my mother's hands like I memorized the rest of her, the milky blue circles around her dark pupils, the hollowed cheeks where the back teeth were missing, the push of her nipples against the nightgown, the smell of her neck when she kissed me on Tuesdays on her way out the door to Julie, perfumed and expectant. I try to imagine Ida sitting here next to me, patting my sweaty head with a tissue, holding my hand as this white-haired lady cradles her son's when he groans and fusses, but the image will not stick. I cannot imagine her being that tender, or me being so helpless in front of her. I cannot imagine her bearing that closeness. Or maybe I'm the one who couldn't. The man is holding his mother's wrists as she pulls him into a seated position. He looks nearly as old as she does, sharp-boned and hunched, crazy-eyed, as she guides the straw between his lips; and yet, he's probably no more than forty. She glances over and sees me watching. Our eyes meet—the old lady smiles. *The bridge between man and God,* I think. That's how a poet defined a smile. She cups the back of his head in her hand, as if he were still the baby she carried, and lowers him gently back into the chair.

· eighteen ·

My fear of having made Ida angry, combined with Sullivan's pushing me to "feel the family out" in person, forces me to make a trip
home. Going to California is an ordeal in the best of times; at the
moment, it's horrible. A psychoanalyst told me once that if you
truly want to test your mental health, go home and see your parents. "An instant rage comes over me," wrote Alfred Kazin of his
own homecomings—crossing the bridge from Manhattan to
Brooklyn to face his family, and his past—"mixed with dread and
some unexpected tenderness." Those are my feelings exactly on
the plane flying west to Los Angeles.

We've agreed to meet at Grandpa's house, and when I pull up
in my rental car, I see that the gang's all here.

"Look at him, Eye!" Aunt Ruth says, taking my hands when I
walk through the door. "He's fine!"

My mother is looking me up and down, tentatively nodding.

Belle has her hands around my waist, squeezing tight. Joyce—who lives the life of a drifter and rarely dares to show her face—has made a surprise appearance and is standing by herself at a distance, visibly out of place. Aunt Ruth pinches my butt. "Give me that *tuchis!*" she says.

"Leave him alone, Ruthie." My mother can't stand to see her love-hungry sister moving in on her kids. "Get over here," she says to me. When I kiss her cheek, it's hollow and cool, and when I hug her, her shoulders won't give; she pats the sides of my arms instead of hugging me back. Her beehive is freshly washed and sprayed, more salt than pepper now, and in spite of her bright pink sweatsuit and lipstick, my mother's color isn't good.

"Say hello to your sister," she says.

Joyce is smiling at me with neglected teeth.

"Hey," I say. "Long time."

"Three years. Right, Mommy?"

"How should I know?"

Joyce comes forward hesitantly and pecks me on the cheek.

Out on the sunporch amidst a jungle of plastic plants, Hadassah plaques, and cases of discount food he drags home from the bulk store, Grandpa is sitting straight-backed in a lawn chair, looking powdery and ancient, with his shirt buttoned to the collar and his hands folded tight in his lap. He beams at me when I kiss him on the mouth, enormous ears standing out from his head like Mom's and mine, round eyes tearing up at the sight of his family all together. His second wife, Emma, with whom he began a long-distance courtship shortly after Bella died, is frantically trying to throw together an impromptu lunch for our visit but seems to have forgotten what she was looking for as she pants

from the porch to the kitchen, then wanders back again. She's gotten heavier since her memory went—she must forget *not* to eat—
and, from the sound of things, is driving Grandpa crazier than
ever.

"What did I come out here for?" Emma asks us. She's stalled
in the doorway, pulling at her beige hair, blinking through her
bifocals like a confused child. "You know, I'm really losing my
marbles."

"She *is*," Grandpa says.

"Shut up, Sidney. Oh, that's what! The tongue."

"She's *meshugah*," Grandpa grumbles, pointing at his temple.

"I heard that!" says Emma, coming back with the slab of
sliced cow mouth. Then she whispers loud in my ear, "At least I
can urinate!"

"Em, please," says Aunt Ruth.

"He stands there for a half hour and nothing comes out,"
Emma tells me.

"It's true," says Grandpa.

"Enough, Dad," says Mom.

"And the gas from these pills!" Emma clutches her stomach
and puffs out her cheeks at me. "They make me belch!"

Joyce lets out one of her stuck-pig squeals that sends Belle and
me into hysterics, just as Joyce's laugh always has, and suddenly
we're like kids again. Mom starts laughing, too, then Emma (who
loves a party), while Joyce holds her nose and tries to stop, her big
face turning scarlet. Aunt Ruth shakes her head like a librarian.
Grandpa is completely lost.

"How about some gefilte fish?" Emma asks me once we've
quieted down. She knows that I have a weakness for pike.

"The prince is home. My wandering Jew." My mother smirks and lights a smoke, then sits back to watch me eat. Seeing food go into my mouth is her idea of great entertainment.

"He looks so much older," Joyce says, as if I were deaf or not sitting right here.

"What's with the hair?" Emma asks, staring at my shaven head.

"I like it this way," I say. Louis has encouraged me to give up the camouflage and razor what's left of my hair to the scalp.

"Why don't you get a toupee?" asks Mom.

"I don't want a toupee," I say.

"Stop it," says Belle. "He looks . . . interesting."

"He looks just like Jim if you ask me," Joyce says. I've heard this ever since I was a boy. Relatives and friends would stare, shake their heads, tell me I was my dad's spitting image. I always found their pronouncements confusing; it's boggling for a kid to be told he's the replica of someone he can't remember. It makes him somehow invisible to himself. Now, Joyce tells me to show her my profile. "See, Mommy, just like Jim."

Mom looks disgusted and tells me to eat.

"What about me?" asks Belle, whose face is narrow and Slavic like mine.

Joyce shakes her head.

"Not at all?"

"You don't want to look like him," Aunt Ruth says.

"Drop it," says Mom.

"Don't they know?" I ask her.

"Know what?" Joyce asks.

"I hired a detective to find him."

The patio goes instantly quiet. Aunt Ruth puts her hand to

her mouth. Grandpa stops chewing and puts down his fork. Joyce mouths *oh, shit*. Mom crushes her butt in a mound of cole slaw.

"Isn't that fantastic?" Belle says.

Grandpa opens his mouth to speak: Emma tells him to mind his own business. Aunt Ruth slowly shakes her head. Mom stands up and goes inside. I take out a pencil and notebook, afraid that I'll forget what they say, and at this moment, I do feel a traitor.

"What do you remember about him?" I ask Joyce, who was twelve when my father left.

"I thought he was the cat's meow."

"Why?"

"'Cause he was a hunk!" she says, licking the mayonnaise off her fingers. "And our dad didn't give a shit. . . ."

"Joyce Anne!" says Aunt Ruth.

"He didn't. But Jim did. Sometimes too much."

I ask Joyce what she means by that.

"Jim wasn't easy. If you didn't do things his way, boom, he went crazy. Perfectionist. Sometimes he hit us. Then again, he could be a big doll."

"Really?"

"Sweet as sugar. We worshipped the ground he walked on. Great sense of humor, but moody. Secretive. You never knew the whole story with him."

Ida returns to her seat and stares at the backyard through the porch screen, her mouth twitching down at the left corner the way it does when she's upset.

"There was something special about your father," says Joyce.

"Especially nuts," Aunt Ruth tells me.

"Passionate. Something different. Right, Mommy?" My mother rolls her eyes. "But then he'd lose control. Like the time he almost broke your neck."

"What?"

"The first time he came back for you."

"First time?"

"He came for you in the middle of the night and took you to a motel." My mother looks like she wants to slap Joyce. "He locked you in a room and said he wouldn't let you out if Mommy didn't give in. But she wouldn't. When the cops came, he threw you down on the bed and almost broke your neck."

"Is that true?" I ask Ida.

She nods.

"What about me?" Belle asks.

"He only wanted Mark," says Joyce, who doesn't know the meaning of tact.

"He wasn't well, honey," Aunt Ruth says quickly, touching Belle's hand. "I think your father had a disease."

"What kind of disease?" Belle asks.

"A mental disease."

"You mean he was crazy?"

"That's my theory."

"Malarkey," my mother says to Aunt Ruth.

"He never paid me back," says Grandpa, who never forgets a nickel. "Jim was a *shicker*. A real nogoodnik."

"Shut up, Sidney," Emma says.

"This is my house and I'll talk if I want to. I don't mean no harm, Mark."

"I know, Grandpa."

"But your father was a liar and a thief."

I feel wounded by this, though I don't doubt it's true, as if they're attacking me and Belle. I want to jump to my father's defense, but what ammunition would I use? I have no proof that he wasn't a sleazebag, yet I'm struck by how unfair it is that in all these years, we've never heard his side of things, the *man's* side. I try to picture a passionate loner, lost in his life, struggling to make his way in the world, tied down to a distant, difficult woman who loved someone else, supporting another man's daughters, coming to the end of his rope. I try to imagine my father not as the cartoon bad guy but as a flawed, confused human being who made a terrible mistake. There must have been details behind his leaving that we will never know; besides, I've wanted to leave myself. There were countless times when I would have abandoned this family if I could have, years when I felt trapped with these people, clawing the walls, waiting for the day I could flee. Sitting here with his enemies, I can even imagine sympathy for someone who managed to free himself—who may have saved his own life by going. Or is this mere defensiveness? Maybe I'm taking his side out of spite; maybe he wasn't a hero at all, but the deadbeat coward they say he is, who ran away without any honor. This question of my father's character, which barely mattered to me in the past, is starting to matter to me now.

"He must have had some virtues," I say.

My mother hesitates then says, "Your father was a sensitive man."

"Sensitive?" I ask.

"Too sensitive for me. I didn't like it."

It's strange to hear this coming from her; for the first time that I can remember, Mom's talking about him without contempt, which makes me brave. "Did you ever love him?" I ask.

"Sure, she loved him," Emma says, forgetting that she never met my father.

"She never loved any of them, I don't think," Aunt Ruth interjects without being asked.

"She loved Julie," Joyce says.

My mother jerks her head to the side at the mention of Julie's name. Then, as if in self-defense, says, "I had feelings for your father. Once upon a time."

When the others are cleaning up in the kitchen, and Grandpa's locked himself in the bathroom, Belle and I sit on the lawn outside. We know each other too well, and see each other too rarely, to waste a minute with small talk.

"You're really okay?" Belle asks, resting her head in my lap.

"Really," I tell her.

"Why do you seem like you're somewhere else?" She's looking at me with her long-lashed brown eyes, stroking my arm with her crooked finger. "Tell me the truth."

"I'm fine."

"You're not."

"I'm worried."

"About what?"

I don't know where to begin, or whether I want Belle to know everything. She's still my baby sister—though twice divorced and a mother of three—it's still my job to try to protect her. Though Belle's grown wise from her own tragedies, and is far more maternal than Mom ever was, to me she'll always be the baby in the incubator, struggling to stay alive; the little girl with stick-thin legs, trailing me through childhood, hanging on my every word; the drug-addled teenager who asked me for help; the adored sister, pretty and frail, who wanted me to be her father.

"I can see that something's wrong."

"The family," I say. "Mom doesn't look good."

"She won't get a checkup. What about you?"

"I'm seeing someone."

"That's good. So tell me."

"Status quo," I say. "Copacetic."

"Thank God." Belle decides to believe me. We're quiet a moment, holding hands, looking at a cloudless sky. The lines in her face are surprisingly deep; Belle looks prematurely aged, but then, we both looked old as children. "Old souls," Yetta used to say, *alte nishomas,* holding our pointed chins in her hands. "Born with the world on your shoulders." Looking down at Belle's face now, I remember Yetta's words. Belle holds my hand and kisses it. "What'll we do if we find him?" she asks.

"No idea."

"It's scary."

"It is."

"What if he hates us?"

"He won't," I say.

"I'm having these weird dreams."

"Me too."

"Maybe it's fate," Belle says. "Don't you believe in fate?"

"That depends what you mean by fate."

"That nothing happens by accident."

"No."

"You think things happen for no reason?"

"Reasons aren't fate," I say. "Reasons can be changed."

"I don't know about that," says Belle. "Maybe we think we're deciding things but really we're just following orders."

"Whose orders?"

"The plan," she says. "I think there's a plan."

"A blueprint, you mean."

"Destiny."

"Ah, destiny. I don't believe in destiny," I say.

"Why not?"

"Life's complex. There's chaos, too."

"I thought that you believed in God."

"God is chaotic."

"But God has a plan."

"Maybe," I say. "Or maybe not."

"I feel like we're meant to look for him now. I feel like it's happening for a reason."

"Maybe you're right."

"Everything's about to break. Don't you feel that? And things will be better afterward."

I say nothing. Belle's smiling. She seems to see good things ahead in her version of fate and reconstruction. I don't want to frighten her. When Mom comes outside to sit on the grass, the conversation turns to dinner. Belle begins to rub her shoulders, and Mom lets out a deep moan. With her eyes closed, my mother reaches out and touches my arm, then pulls her hand back instantly. I have the impulse to touch her back, but don't know where or how. Instead, I watch Belle's twisted finger curl around the back of Mom's neck, massage the top of her head, then work its way along the skull, looking for the pressure points. When Mom starts snoring, Belle winks at me, and leans Mom back on the grass very gently. We watch her ashen face as she sleeps. And I wonder what exactly is breaking.

· nineteen ·

Life came at Belle with open jaws. I tried to protect her but I failed. Before I knew it, the damage was done.

She'd been born prematurely with a hole in her heart, a year before my father left, at a time when my mother's affair with Julie was still in its first bloom. How Belle turned out to be Jim's and not Julie's seems to have been a matter of chance; had Belle been conceived at lunchtime she might have been born with red hair and freckles and not looked like me at all. I stared at her through the nursery window, inside the plastic-domed incubator, scrawny and helpless with a mask over her face, and wondered for weeks if she'd ever come home. She seemed too small to live outside, and when they finally did let her leave, I guarded Belle's crib like a three-year-old soldier, listening for coughs or wheezes, or any other sign that she was in trouble. I lived in fear of losing her, and fantasized often about saving her life. In my nightmares, Belle was always in danger, calling me from somewhere that I couldn't reach; the nights she died in my dreams, I woke up screaming. I'd open my eyes in the morning afraid that Belle would be cold in her crib. Later, when I was the man of the house, this paranoia extended to Mom; no sooner had I woken up than I checked to make sure they were both breathing. With Belle, the job seemed even more urgent; we needed each other as nobody else. Together we were the only proof that our father had ever existed.

Belle was named for Grandma Bella, who'd been buried a few months before Belle was born. Mom showered Belle with all the feeling she'd never been able to show her own mother, loving this new baby more than she loved the rest of us, with the passion of remorse.

"Where did our father go?" Belle asked sometimes.

I would tell her not to think about it.

"Why not?"

"Because I said so."

"Why?"

"Because he's dead," I'd say, repeating Mom's refrain, slamming the door hard to save Belle from hoping, to teach her to adapt as I had.

A fatherless home is a dangerous place. A fatherless home with an absentee mother can seem like it's missing a roof and a floor, like four shaky walls barely fixed to the ground, a door without locks blowing open and closed, letting in far too many strangers. Without protection you can't quite be children; without someone to guard against danger alongside another who's warming the nest, childhood innocence is lost. Visiting friends' homes when I was a boy, I was amazed most of all by the order that held their lives together. I envied their mothers' control of the house, the steady earning hands of their fathers. Two parents seemed to form the axis that kept these normal families in orbit, while ours spun forever out of control. This kept me alert, in a low-grade panic, vigilant for signs of trouble.

The day that trouble came for Belle, though, I'd turned my back and wasn't looking. I was seventeen by then, running after drugs and sex. Joyce was already on the skids, spending time with a derelict crowd she'd met years before at Spawn Ranch, the stable where her high-school friends liked to party, and where Charlie Manson later cooked up his ugly scheme. Joyce would tell us stories about her own freaky gang and the pet monster they kept on the ranch: a three-eyed, four-horned bull, foamy-mouthed and crazy inside a locked pen, with multiple maulings to its credit.

The day I wish had never happened, Joyce took Belle, then fourteen, to visit one of her Spawn friends at a movie-animal training ranch. Belle had been wandering around the grounds, looking at llamas, elephants, bears, lions, camels, and wolves in their pens, when she saw a tiger in the distance, sitting at the back of its cage licking its paws like one of our housecats. Belle had always been fearless with animals, and, with no one around to stop her, she ducked underneath the rope and ran toward the tiger's cage, mesmerized by the cat's golden fur and the amber eyes studying her as she approached.

"Come here, girl," she remembers saying. At first, the tiger stayed where it was, rolling a rubber ball around with the tip of her nose. Belle tapped her wrist against the bars of the cage. "Come on, beautiful. Let's play," she said, then slipped her fingers through the bars and beckoned the tiger to come nearer. The cat ambled over toward where Belle was standing, sniffing inches from her hand.

"Come on," Belle said, reaching further inside the cage and touching the tip of the tiger's wet nose, nearly as big as the palm of her hand. Belle touched the satiny fur by its eyes, then tugged on the long white hairs standing out on its brow.

"Aren't you beautiful," Belle whispered, but before she knew what was happening, the tiger jerked its head around and bit down hard. It happened so fast that Belle made no noise, and when the animal yanked her against the cage, tossing its head from side to side as finger bones crunched inside its jaws, Belle forced out a scream to stop herself from fainting. Excited, the tiger bit down harder, pulling Belle through the bars to her shoulder, champing up toward the elbow. Belle screamed again, and Joyce ran from where she'd been feeding the other animals. The tiger opened its mouth fast, and when Belle saw the bloody tendons and bones, she fainted dead away.

She was in and out of a public ward at County General for the next three months as a parade of second-rate doctors botched her surgeries. Infections came one after the other till three of Belle's fingers were purple and swollen into the shape of claws. Shamed by her deformed hand, she dropped out of school after being discharged and fell in with a bunch of hoodlums—as Mom and Joyce had done before her. In months, the sweet little girl I'd known seemed to disappear, replaced by a low-rider chick wearing too much makeup, too-tight jeans, and a chip on her shoulder that I couldn't budge. She hooked up with a new boyfriend, an illiterate Chicano with homemade tattoos and a Coors belly. When he got her pregnant and asked her to marry him, Belle said, "Why not?"

I wanted to chase him off with a shotgun, the way I imagined a father would, and save her from following in Mom's trashy footsteps, but I had no authority. I begged my mother to intervene, to threaten Belle's suitor with jail time for statutory rape of a minor, but though she was heartbroken at what she saw, fatalism stopped her from acting. "No one could have stopped me," Mom said. "What makes you think that I can stop her?" Perhaps, like Belle, she believed in destiny, or believed that women were condemned by their sex to follow wherever men wanted to pull them, shackled by some kind of primitive law, and the need to be held in masculine arms—engulfed, defined, and overpowered—regardless of what kind of man did the holding. I sat in the church between Mom and Joyce, grinding my teeth as Belle said her vows and accepted the ring on her twisted finger, the other hand resting on her full belly. I never said a word to the groom, and when he deserted Belle a year later, leaving her with an infant son, I felt torn between hope that she'd reclaim her life and the urge to hunt the worm down, murder him with my bare hands for abandoning my baby sister and her newborn son. I wanted to watch him die in cold blood and know that this was old-fashioned justice.

· twenty ·

Sullivan seems to be getting nowhere, but brushes off my worry like lint.

"I'll find him, I'll find him, don't look so gloomy," he says ten weeks into the investigation. He talks to me like a child sometimes, and seems to be comforting me too often, even though I don't expect it. He wants to know more about my background.

"How'd you get into your racket?" he asks with his hands on his head, wing tips crossed on the top of his desk.

"I needed a job. I wanted to write." I tell Sullivan about coming to New York after getting my Master's, working up a few connections, doing stringer work for Reuters, landing a summer job at *Newsweek*, proofreading for Warhol's *Interview*, climbing the masthead to senior editor, quitting to travel around the world and free-lance while I wrote my first book. I make myself sound upwardly mobile—respectable in Sullivan's eyes—and leave out the parts about death and God.

"A self-made man," he says.

"More or less."

"That's good, I respect that. Every connection, every file in this place I got by myself. I earned every penny I've got the hard way," he says, rapping his knuckles against his chest. "It's better that way. It gives you balls."

"No question about it."

"Your old man would be proud of you."

"Thank you for saying so."

I don't like this kind of talk. I want to keep our relationship professional. Besides, I don't need Sullivan's sympathy, I need his radar, which seems to be going on the blink. In spite of his bluster he's coming up dry. The memos keep piling up in the mail, but the names have started to repeat themselves, and I'm starting to wonder if Sullivan is trying to look busier than he is. I don't doubt his expertise—if anyone can find my father, Sullivan can—but maybe there is no warm body. Maybe my mother's wish-fulfilling mantra, *he's dead, he's dead, he's dead,* is a fact after all. The difference is that I'm no longer cavalier about the outcome; I'm determined now to find my father or stand by his grave (if there is one) and mourn. Either way, put an end to this mystery.

"Can't we try something else?" I ask.

"Don't you trust me?"

"Yes, I trust you. But this is starting to wear me down."

Sullivan hesitates then buzzes Liz.

"What!" she squawks from the other room.

"Get me the sob-story file." Moments later, Liz appears with a large envelope and hands it to her boss. "What took you so long?" he asks.

"You're *welcome*," Liz says. "Can I get you something else? A Prozac?"

"Two," says Sullivan, winking at me. "With a chaser." When Liz shuts the door, he hands me something that looks like a government application. "I don't like to do this," he says, explaining that the Freedom of Information Office in Washington, D.C., a subdivision of the Department of Health and Human Services, offers a venue for finding missing persons for people in life-threatening situations. The words *life-threatening* stop my reading. How much does Sullivan know? He's watching me with his sky-blue eyes, hands folded across his belly, hair backlit like a milky halo. Is he acting so fatherly, I wonder, because he suspects that I'm not well? I try to put this out of my mind.

Sullivan explains the procedure, which requires writing my father an open letter which will then be screened by the Office for extortion threats and other libelous contents, and then will be forwarded by "inside means" should James J. Matousek be found. Sullivan dislikes this route since it runs the risk of tipping off the suspect, allowing him to take deeper cover. But since we seem to be losing steam, he says it might be worth a shot.

"You mean a last resort?" I ask.

"Probably not."

"What should I say?"

"Make something up. Rip his heart out. You're a writer. Make him weep." Sullivan shows me to the door. "And make sure you put a picture in. Show the son of a bitch what he's missing."

I put off writing the letter for days. When I finally sit down to
write it, I don't know what salutation to use or the appropriate
tone with which to address him. I try a number of dead-end ap-
proaches—too earnest, casual, stiff, or needy:

> *Dear Father: It's important that I meet with you as soon as
> possible for reasons that will soon be clear. . . .*

> *Hey Dad, Just thought I'd say hello and find out what you're
> up to after all this time! I thought it might be fun to
> talk. . . .*

> *Dear James Matousek: I realize that this letter will surprise
> you, and hope that it finds you in good health. Although we
> do not know each other, and may not wish to, I wanted to
> make some effort. . . .*

> *Dear Daddy, Please write to me as soon as you get this. I'm
> feeling confused about so many things and could really use
> some advice. . . .*

I tear up draft after draft, surprised that I can't seem to find
the right voice with which to introduce myself. Faced with the
prospect of speaking to him, it's as if I have no voice at all. I'm
powerless and mute as a dummy without a ventriloquist. I start
and stop for over an hour, struggling to invent the voice of a son
my father might actually want to know, someone intriguing yet

independent, eager yet unthreatening. I want to pique his interest without seeming desperate, hook him as he's begun to hook me. The fact that the letter will be read by strangers makes this seduction even trickier. What's needed is a coded plea, but I can't seem to pull it off. Finally, I run out of patience and opt for dullness:

Dear Father,

I hope that you're well. It's been so many years since we've seen each other. I realize that this letter will surprise you, but I hope it doesn't make you unhappy. Let me assure you that I hold no grudge against you whatsoever, neither does Belle Lynn, who now has three little boys and has always hoped to see you again. The boys would also like to meet their grandfather.

Please understand that we want nothing from you except your good wishes, should you feel comfortable enough to contact us. What's more, there's no need to inform our mother of your response, or whereabouts, if this would bother you. I'm undergoing treatment for a serious illness but feel fine and hope to beat it. Maybe we'll even be able to meet.

That's all I wanted to say. Whatever happens, please know that I remember you with fondness, and hope that life has been good to you.

Yours sincerely,
Mark Matousek

Once I've squeezed these paragraphs out, Louis helps me look for a photo. We sit on the floor surrounded by all the pictures I have, from kindergarten to adolescence to pictures published in magazines. Once again, I feel overwhelmed. Summing up three decades of life in a single camera click is as hard as finding the right tone of voice. Sifting through these images, I'm filled with an aching regret that my father never saw me grow up; incredibly, our mutual, irrevocable loss strikes me for the first time. If Jim Matousek is alive, and thinks of me at all, all he could remember is a skinny, snaggle-toothed bundle of trouble. He never knew what came afterward—hopeless Cub Scout, Ajax-haired surfer, Eurail backpacker, hotshot reporter. It seems dishonest—wasteful, in fact—to reduce life to one snapshot, to fast-forward into middle age and erase all the years, and characters, that one has lived through before. But short of sending a full chronology, I have no choice. After long deliberation, I choose an image from more prosperous times, slip it into an envelope, and mail it with my letter to a bureaucrat in Washington.

· twenty-one ·

I started to write compulsively when I was in the second grade, journals full of secret thoughts and shameful truths that I could tell no one. This isn't an uncommon way to begin; lots of writers turn inward as children to stop themselves from going crazy. These notebooks were my confessional, the secret place where I could bear witness, reveal myself fully and come to admit what I hoped for the future. I could tell the whole truth in this private place, ground myself in a shaky world, render the minutes and hours and days—the fleeting, dissolving wonder of things—substantial on paper if nowhere else. I needed to tell *the real story* somewhere. If more than a day passed without recording what I saw and felt, I began to disappear. Life bunched up like a broken-reeled movie; voices and visions twisted inside me. My camera, my eye, my *I*, went dark. Without the lens of words on a page, proof that I was alive and watching, I grew frantic.

Reading the diaries of prisoners later, I felt as if I were a prisoner, too, who shared their need for evidence. After reading Anne Frank's diary at eleven, I felt as if she were a kindred soul. I imagined her locked in a silent attic, filling pages to help her survive. She knew that life in that hidden place would be forgotten without her pen; she knew that her struggle, and that of her family, would count for nothing without a record. She wrote so as not to lose her mind, and though I wasn't a prisoner like she was, I did feel trapped as a boy by a darkness that threatened to snuff me out. I needed to know what our family was hiding, and what had gone so dreadfully wrong here; why my mother's will seemed so broken, why my father never came back, why Marcia lay hidden under her bedsheets, why Joyce gorged herself until she couldn't walk, where the God I saw worshipped elsewhere had dissolved to, leaving us the local pariahs. But my questions were met with shoulder shrugs, blank looks, irritation or anger. Mom compared me to the Gestapo; Joyce ignored me; Marcia tried to explain things sometimes but her answers seemed either naïve or false, watered-down pabulum to a child as gimlet-eyed as I was.

Thus, receiving no credible answers, I wrote and wrote, filling spiral binders and notepads and loose-leaf pages, napkins, postcards, and strips of toilet paper. Reams of confusion and threats and confessions, raging, shameful observations lay stored in a box underneath my bed. I analyzed till I started to see; words could sometimes cut through the shadows, make order from chaos, turn me into a different person, akin to myself or someone stronger. The voice I wrote with wasn't my mother's; it sounded like a man's voice on paper, reasoned, fearless, steady, clear. Nailed down by language, confusion could turn to certainty. Words became powerful instruments, shovels for digging up secrets and holding them up to newfound light—blades for cutting through the dark, hammers for pounding tumultuous life into solid, beautiful stories.

I wrote everywhere: in the coat closet at school, behind the handball court during recess, in the parking lot behind the liquor store, out back on the lawn at home, at the neighborhood library, at the kitchen table, on the back seat of Mom's T-bird, in bed, on the toilet, in the bathtub, waiting at the barber shop. I was so absorbed by my hand's movement, the syllables forming in my mind, the scenes I drew, and the talk I remembered, that I often forgot where I was, or who might be watching me. In the B volume of the World Book Encyclopedia that Mom bought on layaway from a traveling salesman, I read in the section on bullfighting about the *querencia,* the invisible power zone in the ring where the animal was safe from the people trying to kill it. "As if by magic," the World Book said, "the *querencia* protects the bull from the matador's taunts and seduction." I'd sit in my favorite spot in the middle of the living-room rug, notebook balanced on crossed legs, and think of that spot as my *querencia,* the magical power place where no one could touch me or stop me or hurt me. I'd watch the family move around me—Belle sleeping spoons with a kitten on the couch, Marcia shimmying to Chubby Checker, my mother pouring her heart out to Yetta, one foot in the widow's lap as her corns came off with cuticle scissors— as if from behind a one-way mirror, recording precisely what I saw, down to the crumb. My happiest moments were spent this way, preventing us—it seemed to me—from being forgotten without a trace, disappearing into oblivion.

. . .

"He has quite an imagination," Mrs. Caprio said.

It was the second semester of second grade and my homework assignments had gotten completely out of hand. When the class was assigned a one-page essay about our favorite animal, I turned in ten pages describing how cats were taking over the world (there were seven in our apartment alone) and how we should institute a global policy of feline euthanasia. Mrs. Caprio was alarmed enough to call my mother in for a special conference.

"Quite an imagination," she said again.

Mom smiled. I was ashamed of her teeth, and the black wool coat she was wearing, down to her calves, even though the sun was out.

"But I must say, Mrs. Matousek . . ."

"Ida."

". . . there are disturbing elements." I remember Mrs. Caprio leafing through my most recent composition and showing it to Mom with a flourish. "Cats, like women, can be dangerous," she read. "Their feces alone can carry disease." She turned to me. "Now what is that supposed to mean?"

I told her that it was poetic license.

"Oh, really?" said Mrs. Caprio, who had orange hair and a face like a turnip. "You see what I mean, Mrs. . . . . Ida?"

"I don't know where he gets it," Mom said.

I seem to remember chiming in that I got *it* from my father. Mrs. Caprio liked to split hairs, and said she'd been given to understand that I didn't have a father.

"Everyone has a father," I said.

"In the *home*," she said.

"I'm divorced," Mom told her.

Mrs. Caprio looked sympathetic. "That must be terribly hard on you. Being two parents. Especially for a boy."

"I handle it." Mom disliked interference.

"That's why I thought we should find him an outlet," said Mrs. Caprio. I heard Mom thinking, *not if it costs money,* but the teacher produced an entry form for a state essay contest for kids under twelve. The winner of the contest would be invited to read his essay on TV, then make an appearance on Art Linkletter's House Party. Mrs. Caprio seemed to think I had a chance, if I stayed away from what she called *a certain tone.*

As it happened, my certain tone suited the topic perfectly: an essay about Baba Yaga, the hag in the Russian fairy tale who lives in a house on stilts in the middle of the forest, eating small children. Using our neighbor Mrs. Sims as a model, I wrote an extended meditation on the cannibal witchwoman who'd long inhabited my psyche, describing how "her mollusk-like nose protruded, hair-filled, from her hideous face." I took home first prize and read the essay on an educational television show the following week, with shaking hands and sweat running down the middle of my back.

Although Mrs. Caprio was as proud as a stage mother that I'd won, she seemed less than overjoyed by the impression I'd made on the small screen, and rehearsed with me after school, in preparation for Art Linkletter. Her humiliating instructions have remained with me all these years.

"Be sure to keep your hands in your lap," she said, fingers folded primly in the cleavage between her thighs. "Too much gesticulation confuses the camera." What Mrs. Caprio really meant was, don't fling your wrists around like a fruitcake, but I was too young to grasp her meaning.

"How can you confuse a camera?" I asked.

"It's a figure of speech," she explained.

"I don't get it."

"Just keep your hands in your lap, please!"

"I'll try not to move."

"And don't bat your eyes."

"What do you mean?"

Mrs. Caprio blinked like a spastic.

"I twitch when I'm nervous. I can't help it."

"The camera dislikes it."

I promised that I'd try to stop.

The day of the taping, Mom and I drove on the freeway to CBS and parked at a far end of the lot where no one would see our dilapidated car. By the time we arrived, I was sick with stagefright and the smell of Aqua Net hairspray. After wandering around in search of the soundstage, we finally found the right door, and Mom gave me a kiss before finding her seat in the audience. I could see how nervous she was—everyone we knew would be watching. At school, Mrs. Caprio had called an assembly, with a TV set up in the auditorium. "Please don't be a smartass," she warned.

Backstage, the other three kids and I were prepped with questions by a friendly woman who told us what Art was going to say and asked us what we intended to answer.

"I thought this was. . . ." I searched for the word that meant impromptu. "Not planned," I said.

"It's not. Not *really*. We just like to have some idea of what you might say and make suggestions."

"Why?"

"Because Mr. Linkletter likes it that way."

This was my first peek into show business fakery and the realization that things on TV were far from what they seemed. This disillusionment was cinched when a tall man wearing pumpkin-colored makeup came into the room and winked at the lady doing the prepping. His wispy hair was dyed the same color as his face. Then I realized that it was Art Linkletter.

"And who are *you?*" he asked in loud voice, bending over to stare at my face.

"Mark," I said, shaken by how strange he looked, and how weird it was that a famous person could step through the screen into three dimensions.

"You gonna be funny, Mark? You gonna make us laugh?"

"I'll try," I said.

"He'll try!" Linkletter guffawed like I'd said the stupidest thing in the world. The woman laughed along with him, while the other kids looked gleeful, as if I'd proved what a dummy I was, and ruined my chances of being a hit.

"You do that, Mike," said Art Linkletter.

"Mark."

"Whatever!" He spoke to the others then left the room with the list of questions and answers.

Art Linkletter made me mad. Once the four of us were seated on high-legged director's chairs on the dark stage, before the cameras started rolling, I decided that if Art Linkletter wanted to make a fool of me, I'd make a fool of him first. By the time the blinding lights came up in our faces, revealing the studio audience, my nervousness had worn off and I was ready to flip his lid.

When Art put his hand on my shoulder and introduced me, I avoided looking him in the eye and smiled at the audience.

"What's the naughtiest thing you ever did?" he asked.

"Mooned a nun," I said.

The audience howled. Art's eyes popped out. The other kids giggled. I was supposed to say "put a dead spider in my mother's mascara."

"She liked it," I said.

More laughs from the bleachers. A man in a coat and tie shook his head at me vigorously from behind the camera.

"Is he trying to tell me something?" I asked, but Art had already yanked the mike. When it came time for the next question, he reminded me that there were Christians in the audience. "I'm sure they've seen their share of rear ends. How do you think they get all those kids?"

"Mike—"

"Mark!" Art was getting flustered. I saw the gap between his dentures and gums, and the reds of his eyes when he shot a look at the wide-eyed assistant offstage.

"Aren't you going to ask me a question?"

"What's the worst part about being a kid?"

"Finding go-go girls to sleep with you."

Art threw his hands up in the air and the audience went nuts. The other kids were out of their depth; even though they tried improvising, they couldn't get a laugh. When Art tried skipping me on a question, I asked if he'd forgotten me.

"How could I?"

"So let me have it."

"What do your parents do to liven up a party?"

"Put Spanish flies in the rum and coke."

The audience gasped. Art looked like he wanted to slap me. "Where are this boy's parents?" he shouted.

The cameras panned to Mom in the second row, covering her face with her hands.

"You could use a good licking," he said to me over the commotion.

"I'll bet you could, too," I replied.

My mother was not amused, and neither was Mrs. Caprio, but I became a hero at school. Guys who wouldn't talk to me before now invented the Linkletter Lick—sliding their tongues back and forth like snakes—and wherever I went for the next few weeks, I was greeted with slurps and pats on the back by the boys who never picked me for kickball. Suddenly, girls seemed to think I was cute, and pulled me into their circles to gossip. I was popular at school for the first and last time and amazed that this came from being a writer.

· twenty-two ·

"He's gonna be a *faigelah,* Eye."

Yetta was talking to Mom as she cut up flanken for her borscht. I was sitting on Yetta's plastic-covered couch looking through her knitting magazines, eating orange jellies from an antique glass candy-jar on the coffee table, eavesdropping. "A boy needs a father, Eye," she said. "It's not right he should be with girls all the time. He'll start to turn."

"He's fine," Mom snapped to shut her up.

"He's fine but he's funny," the fat lady said.

"Mind your own business."

Nobody criticized Mom's kids but her, and God help anyone who laid a hand on us. That very semester, my third-grade teacher Mr. Katz had mistakenly bent me over for a paddling in his office after my best friend, Barry (The Pygmy) Schlossberg, picked his nose during the freeze bell. When I told my mother what had happened, she stormed into Mr. Katz's office and threatened to have him arrested if he ever touched me again. The widow knew better than to get involved, but she couldn't help being a yenta.

"I know there's nothing *wrong* with him," Yetta said, whacking the beef into bite-sized cubes and dropping them into the pan to sizzle. "I love him, he's adorable, you know that," she said. "I'm just saying that you should be careful."

From that day on, the seed was planted in my mother's head that unless she found me a father figure, I'd be lip-synching *Over the Rainbow* in public before she could say "homosexual." Although she protested—too often—about how much better off I was that my father was gone, about how I wasn't *his kind of boy,* how the son of a bitch would have made my life a living hell—it was obvious how guilty she felt that I didn't have a man around to teach me things that I should be learning, and stop me from getting too light in the loafers. It was obvious from the wisecracks she made about fruits and fairies and faggots and sissies that my mother preferred what she called *a man's man,* with bulging arms like Willy the butcher's. I heard her whispering to Marcia and Joyce that maybe Yetta was right to worry about my needing a man to look up to. This was, after all, the mid-nineteen-sixties, when most people still thought that nurture dwarfed nature, that lifestyle was chosen, and absent fathers promised queer sons. My mother seemed to believe that if some man could teach me to tie a slip knot, flaunt my pecs, and fart without blushing, she could stop me from going wrong. But first she needed a man to help her.

Since Grandpa was out of the question, the task fell to Aunt Ruth's husband Marty, a cuddly, sarcastic galumph of a man who had no more interest in mentoring me than I had in waking at five A.M. to go fishing with him on the San Pedro pier. I protested to no avail, feigning homework and stomachaches, but finally ran out of excuses. The morning of the dreaded day, I sat in the living room before dawn, waiting for Uncle Marty's Corvair, furious at my mother and the world for subjecting me to this stupid ordeal. We drove to the ocean without speaking, listening to big band music on the car radio. When we reached the pier, I followed his quick-moving bulk through the cold air, fishing pole in hand, till an enormous black barge rose out of the fog like the deathship in Treasure Island. Along the decks, loud men and boys, and the occasional brooding female, were scattered at the railings in slickers and sweatshirts, rods outstretched, inspecting the catch in their neighbors' buckets.

Finding an empty spot at the rail, Uncle Marty showed me how to gear up my pole, guide the clear plastic line through the rings, then knot it around a silver hook he handed me from between his teeth. Then he plunged his hand into the bait tank and emerged with two wriggling smelt in his fist. Holding the silver fish close to my face, he jabbed the hook through the top of its head as its body thrashed and eyes poked out, then handed me the other smelt. Fingers shaking, I dropped the squirming fish on the deck, then another and a third, while my uncle shook his head in disgust. Finally, I managed to hold one but couldn't stick the hook through its head. I asked Uncle Marty to do it for me but he refused.

"Pay attention," he said, de-hooking his traumatized fish, squashing it underneath his boot and pulling a new victim up from the tank. He held the smelt even closer this time as it whipped and twisted for dear life, gills pumping, then gouged in the hook with a sadistic laugh. He told me that fish were cold blooded and could not feel pain. I imagined gouging his neck with a cleaver and hanging him over the side of the boat to see what temperature *his* blood was. Instead, I pointed my rod out over the railing at the gray expanse, and counted the minutes till it was over.

By noon, Uncle Marty had caught eight fish, while my bucket contained one shoe-sized bonito. "Not bad for the first time," he said to me, although I sensed that he hated my guts. I'd accidentally let out a scream when the fish fell off the end of the pole and flip-flopped against my foot. Uncle Marty looked furious then and told me I needed some toughening up. This meant, I knew, that he wanted to slap me. When at last the lunch horn blew, he picked up his bucket and then mine, and dumped the tortured fish overboard.

"Why did you do that?" I asked, shocked that we'd killed all those creatures for nothing and angry that I couldn't show Mom my catch.

Uncle Marty wiped his stinking hands on his pants and picked up his tackle box. "Bad eating," he said.

Mom's second attempt to find me a father figure came through my counselor at Camp Max Strauss, Avi Hirshenbein. Camp Max Strauss was a Jewish-run facility in the Angeles National Forest, where she sent me kicking and screaming for two weeks every June. The kids were mostly black, Hispanic, and trailer trash: I was always the only Jew in my cabin. Avi Hirshenbein, who had athletic legs and was studying to be a doctor, took a special interest in me because of the chronic bedwetting that haunted me through my childhood. Hanging my sopping sleeping bag out to dry from a tree near the cabin every morning, for all the boys to see and laugh at, Avi told me that bedwetting was nothing to be ashamed of; in fact, it was a sign of intelligence, and he used to do it himself.

"It's a man's way of holding on to his turf," Avi told me.

I had too much of a crush on Avi, and liked this interpretation too much, to ask him what it meant when girls did it. I told Avi that nearly every night, I dreamt that I was on the can and woke up smelly and wet.

"You see, imagination!" said Avi, putting an arm around my shoulder while the other boys snickered from a distance. "There's nothing to be embarrassed about. You're just different. And they're just jealous."

When our two weeks of mountain climbing, campfire stories, and frigid group showers were over, Avi took my mother aside and told her about the Jewish Big Brothers, a club that matched up fatherless boys with charitable men for weekend outings. I begged Mom not to bother, but she was determined to find me a man and nip my inversion in the bud. She arranged for a Jewish Big Brother named Henry to start taking me out that August, when I was eleven and a half.

It turned out that I liked Henry. He was a sweet, little, bald European who looked like Menachem Begin and told me stories about what it was like to be my age in the Nazi death camps.

"My mama-she-should-rest-in-peace hid in a pile of dead bodies for three days," Henry told me while we ate ice cream at the Tastee-Freez shortly after we met. "Then she moved to Israel and got killed. You never know what's around the corner. You're a lucky boy to have a mother."

I shrugged. "If you say so."

"Someday when God forbid she isn't here anymore you'll look back and remember all the things you should have told her."

"I talk to her but she doesn't talk back."

"Everybody's different," said Henry. "But still you gotta pay her respect. No matter what she does, she still brought you into this world. She's still your mother."

"What about your father?" I asked. We were in the front seat of Henry's old Rambler, heading toward the Griffith Park Zoo.

This time, Henry shrugged.

"Didn't you ever know him?" I asked.

"I knew him." Henry grew very quiet. "You shouldn't have to know from these things."

"You mean they killed him?"

Henry nodded.

"That's sad."

"Life's sad, *boychik*. For everyone sometimes."

"I know."

"It's sad and you go on." Henry let out a long sigh. I'd never seen a man so sad before.

"I like you, Henry," I said.

He looked at me and patted my hand. "I like you, too," said Henry. "My boy don't like to hear these things, all he wants is more toys. You let me talk."

"I like to listen."

"For that I'll teach you another song!" He'd already taught me a song that I liked, a Hebrew coffee-drinking song which I'd sung at home till my sisters were frantic. "Interested?"

"Sure, I am."

Henry turned off the radio. Then he began to sing, but this time the tune was mournful and slow. "Oh, *mein* papa," sang Henry in creaky Yiddish tones. "To me he was so wonderful. Oh *mein* papa, to me he was so good." He sang these lines over and over till the old car was full with those bittersweet words and I'd picked up the melody.

"Oh, *mein* papa, to me he was so good," we sang, and in that moment, chugging along in the slow lane of the Hollywood Freeway, past the mortuary where Grandma Bella was buried, on our way to the zoo in the front seat of Henry's old Rambler, I felt closer to him than I'd ever felt to a grown man, because he was sad and gentle and kind—and odd, like me, in his sandals and white socks, eyeglasses held together with Scotch tape, shiny bald head, and thin white arms wisped with hair like a woman's.

I looked forward to Saturdays with Henry, but after a dozen afternoons, seeing movies, exploring the park, reading together in the library where Henry showed me Anne Frank's diary, he stopped coming. Henry told me how sorry he was, but he was having trouble at home and needed to spend more time with his own son. Mom seemed as upset as I was, and called Henry again herself, asking him to please reconsider. Henry just told her that he couldn't help it; his wife didn't like him seeing me after all, though Henry never told Mom why. When she offered to find me another Big Brother, I threatened to run away from home. I'd already done it once in third grade, and Ida knew that I'd do it again. She had to face the fact that she couldn't save me from having no father, or straighten me out like a wire hanger. I was bent and that was that, and though my mother resented this, and felt betrayed by nature for giving her that kind of boy, she never once said this out loud. Instead she surrendered to what could not be changed, defended me against mocks and taunts, and buried her disappointment in silence.

· twenty-three ·

There's a message on the answering machine from Mac Sullivan. "Call me immediately. I have good news."

When I'm finally able to reach him on his car phone, Sullivan sounds excited. A James J. Matousek with an Illinois Social Security number issued at roughly the time of my father's birth has turned up somewhere in California. When I press Sullivan for details, he's cagey about the suspect's exact whereabouts and tells me that he needs to do reconnaissance before saying more.

"What kind of reconnaissance?" I ask.

"Snooping around."

"What if it's him?"

"Then we have to make sure that he's surrounded."

"He's not a criminal," I say, but technically this isn't true. In the eyes of the world, in the eyes of the law, in the eyes of nearly everyone but me, my father is a criminal, the worst sort of deadbeat human being. And yet there's a marked discrepancy between this consensus view and the story I've managed to tell myself about my father's heroic escape, and how much he really wanted me. If that were completely true, however, why did he give up so easily? Why, unless he was dead, has he never once contacted me when our phone number has always been listed? How have I managed to convince myself, in spite of his track record, that he wouldn't just slither away like a snake if Mac Sullivan kicked his rock? I realize—again—what a fiction I've built to excuse my father's abandoning us, protecting myself by turning him noble. And yet, I know that Sullivan's right. If my father is alive, he's nearly seventy by now and might not be eager to trip with me down memory lane or face the prospect of legal trouble. Three decades' worth of guilt might well prompt him to disappear. Though I'd like to think better of Pasadena Jim (as Sullivan dubs him after this, giving me some clue of his location), the detective is wise to expect the worst.

"How do you stop him from escaping?"

"Get his neighbors to keep an eye on him. Get a fix on his license plate. See about family, friends, job."

"That takes how long?"

"This isn't an exact science."

"I know."

"Whoops, I'm in a tunnel."

"Days? Weeks?"

"I'm doing my best." Then Sullivan's voice is drowned out by static.

· twenty-four ·

The man with the scar, across the courtyard, is having sex with a woman his age—forty-five, more or less—who's wearing a black bra and hoop earrings. She's pressed up against the window. I don't think they know that I'm watching. He's behind her, kissing her neck; her hands are wrapped backward over her head, her mouth is open, her eyes closed. She seems to be talking nonstop as he pushes her against the glass, pulls her back, cups her breasts, bites his bottom lip. I like the way women look during sex; it's been years since I made a woman come. Whenever I talk about women to Louis, and tell him how sometimes I miss women's bodies, the smalls of their backs, the taste of lipstick, ponytails, oversized nipples, hospitable entry, soft eyes fixed on yours as you fuck them, he calls me a closet heterosexual. I tell him that I'm not one or the other, that sexuality isn't a box defining us rigidly. People like different things, I suggest, at different times, for different reasons. Beauty's beauty where I'm concerned, and women—despite what the queer police claim—possess certain qualities men never can. I stopped dating women in my twenties only when it became too complex; though I learned that desire obeyed no fixed boundaries, emotional ties proved less flexible, and after a number of tortured triangles with partners of opposites sexes, I saw that a choice was necessary. The man's back is turned to the window now—the women in black has dropped out of sight. I can't see quite what she's doing, but I can imagine with great pleasure.

Though Mom failed to find me a willing role model, I assumed from what she and others said—and from what I observed watching Agent 007 pounce on every vixen he met—that being a man meant having sex, the more the better, with anyone willing to drop their pants. Between eleven and thirteen, nothing obsessed me more than other people's naked bodies. I turned into the neighborhood lecher, persuading kids of both sexes to let me have my way, feeling more powerful with every conquest. Michelle, the girl my mother baby-sat from the time I was seven, was my favorite playmate. She'd become like a fourth sister and trailed along with me wherever I went. We piled curled caterpillars in coffee cans, pulled shy brown spiders from the webs they made under our windowsills, and went to the empty lot behind the JCPenney with beer cans for trapping lizards. When we were bored on long afternoons, Michelle would let me touch her all over as long as I didn't tell anyone.

One day, her panties were down and her biscuit was exposed, soft and white as dough, with a gentle cleft down the middle. When I touched it with my finger, she squirmed. Her powdery mound was sweet and smooth, innocent and all mine. I knew I shouldn't be touching it but didn't even try to resist.

"Look," I said. I'd smuggled one of my mother's *True Confessions* magazines inside my shirt. Inside the smutty tabloid were drawings of half-naked people, women with heaving bosoms and shirtless men with open belts. Michelle looked at the pictures, not knowing what to make of them. I flipped to the story about the cruel gaucho from Argentina, which I'd read over and over. The illustration showed a masked man on his rearing stallion, whip in the air, a bare-breasted woman cowering underneath him in the dust, petticoats to the wind, an outlined tear seeping from one wide blue eye. The handsome gaucho, lord of the pampas, had a face I associated with my father, in the way I'd idealized Mom to look like the MGM lady holding a torch before the credits. The suntanned man on horseback dominated whomever he pleased, roaming wherever his spirit took him.

I opened my fly and Michelle screamed. I'd never shown her mine before, and the little thing seemed to scare her.

"Touch it," I said.

"No!" she squealed.

"I command you!" I said, thinking of the powerful gaucho.

Michelle refused, locking her hands behind her back. When I tried to wrestle them loose, she started screaming. I didn't hear Mom till she was already there, towering over us in her curlers.

"What the hell's going on here?"

"We're playing," I said, yanking my hand from Michelle's underpants. I could tell Mom was acting mad for her ward's sake but was really holding back a smile. She grabbed me by the arm and pulled me up out of the ivy. Michelle scampered away and when she was gone, Mom dusted the dirt off my shorts and pinched my butt.

"Little pistol," she said.

Marcia decided that it was time for Mom to tell me about sex. I told her I'd already learned enough from Dr. David Reuben's *Everything You Always Wanted to Know About Sex*, which I'd filched from the library, along with *Candy* and *The Story of O*. I not only understood the basics but had absorbed more than an eleven-year-old needed to know about ben-wah balls, French ticklers, and The Whipped Cream Flick. Still, Marcia insisted that we have a talk, so the three of us sat around the kitchen table, shut the door so Belle couldn't hear, and opened the World Book to R for reproduction.

Marcia pointed to the diagrams. "Do you understand how the different parts work?"

"It's pretty obvious," I said.

"Is this necessary?" Mom asked.

"It's important," said Marcia. "Who else can he talk to?"

"No one talked to me," said Mom.

Marcia gave her a look that said *we'd all be better off if they had.*

"I know what I'm doing."

"What do you mean doing?"

"With sex," I said.

"You are not having sex."

I smiled to rile her up. I wasn't having sex, per se, but my backyard dates with Rima Louise had progressed to finger insertion.

"You can't have sex at eleven years old."

"Says who?"

"Says me," she replied. But Mom lacked the virtue to put her foot down. When it came to sexual matters, her authority was nonexistent. Besides her taste for *True Confessions,* the lazy susan was filled with matchbooks she'd brought home from her motel dates with Julie. My mother's stabs at being parental often seemed absurd to me, but this was rank hypocrisy.

"Sex should come from love," Marcia said, recalling the hippies we'd seen on TV cavorting naked in Max Yasgur's mudpits and using love power to change the world. "When you love somebody, sex can be something beautiful."

"How?" I asked.

"More than just a physical thing."

I listened to Marcia carefully. She might be naïve but I trusted her and this was truly interesting. Mom seemed interested as well.

"But first you have to care for someone. If you go too fast, it means nothing after."

"Your sister's right," Mom surprised me by saying.

"But most men never learn that," said Marcia.

"They think with their you-know-whats," said Mom.

"They *think* with it?"

"They don't love," said Marcia. "But you can be different," she assured me. "A different kind of man in life."

"Okay," I said without understanding. I wanted her to be proud of me, and Mom too if that was possible. But I didn't want to be any more *different* than I already was.

· twenty-five ·

When I was eight days old, I was strapped to a breadboard and cir-
cumcised on my Aunt Ruthie's kitchen table. There's disagree-
ment among my family about who it was that became ill—it was
either my father or Uncle Marty—but *someone's* castration complex kicked in and sent him retching out of the room when the
mohel tossed my foreskin into a pouch and bandaged my mo-
lested thimble. Marcia let me suck on her finger, dipped into
sweet red wine; my mother drank a toast to the mohel and said
that if he cut off too much, she'd track him down and cut off *his.*
Aunt Ruth cleared the table and wiped down the breadboard.
Lunch was served.

Although we were Jews, we weren't *real* Jews, the kind we
sped by on our bikes on Saturdays as they walked with hats and
strollers to temple. We were fallen Jews, California Jews, indis-
tinguishable, except for the occasional Yiddish, from the *goyim.*

What Jewishness meant in Mom's house was that we ate as much pork as we could digest, got extra days off from school, and decorated a Styrofoam Star of David at Christmastime instead of a tree. At Passover, Grandpa stood at the end of the table, rocking in his tallis and yarmulke, reciting prayers that no one understood, while we fidgeted. My mother sucked on her cigarette, flicking ashes into the palm of her hand.

"Enough already, for Chrissakes, Dad," she'd say when we got to the ten plagues. "Flies, locusts, cattle disease," she'd mutter, as we dipped our pinkies into the wine and dripped it, scourge by scourge, onto Emma's good china.

God was a non-issue in suburbia, something we didn't think about, like Bigfoot. We worshipped in front of the TV set, gave alms at the go-cart track, did our penance at Sears and Roebuck. I remember having spiritual stirrings, an intuition of some higher order, a yearning for wonder and sacredness, but these feelings had nothing to do with religion. My mother rejected God out of hand; Judaism was synonymous with *father* to her—SIDNEY KAPLAN writ large on the walls of a stifling temple of judgment and guilt—though she couldn't deny her *Jewishness*. In spite of this lack of religion, however, there was no doubt that I would have a bar mitzvah when I turned thirteen. Not only did Grandpa insist upon it, but Mom wanted to keep the peace. I liked the whole idea from the start, of a ritual day when I would become a man (and get lots of gifts for my maturation). I liked the idea of ritual, period, anything tied to roots and tradition that might make our family respectable, and bring me into the tribe.

Grandpa enrolled me in a bar mitzvah crash course. Three days a week, he dropped me off at Temple Mishkin Israel, a storefront next to a Chinese takeout on a nearby boulevard, and I spent an hour repeating the tape-recorded version of scripture that Rabbi Shlimkin had given me to memorize. I couldn't understand a word of what I was reading, but the rabbi, a kindly man with lousy breath and a lacquered combover, seemed impressed that I'd taught myself to read along with the advanced edition of the Torah printed without the vowels underneath the letters.

"He could be a cantor, Sid," Rabbi Schlimkin told Grandpa one day. "I'd say he deserves a better Hebrew education."

"I agree with you, Rabbi. But his mother does not keep a kosher home. And she married a *shagitz*."

"What's a *shagitz*?" I asked.

"A non-Jew," the rabbi said.

"My father converted," I said. "Besides, if the mother's Jewish, the child's Jewish. That's the law."

Rabbi Shlimkin patted my head. "You see, Sid? A bright boy."

"Bright, yes," Grandpa said. "But a troublemaker."

"Is that true?" Rabbi Shlimkin asked me.

"No," I said.

"A boy needs a father," Grandpa said.

"It's true, Sid, he does. That's why he needs us." Rabbi Shlimkin put his arm around me. "The world is falling apart, Moishe"—that was the Hebrew name he gave me—"but men like you can save it if you use this." The rabbi tapped my head with his knuckles.

"What about this?" I tapped my chest, thinking about what Marcia had said.

"The heart is the seat of the mind, Moishe. You can't use one without the other. Isn't that right, Sidney?"

Grandpa nodded, clearly out of his depth.

"This is wisdom according to scripture. Two parts make a whole. Remember that in life, my boy. This is how you become a man."

On the morning of my big day, a terrible thunderstorm flooded the valley. Guests arrived at the temple dripping and cursing, umbrellas and plastic bags over their heads. Grandpa and Mom flanked the front door greeting people as they sloshed in. My mother was wearing a new dress and a sassy new flip in her hairdo; I was hiding behind a screen, sweating like a pig in my rented black suit, the verses of the *Shema* going through my brain like a skipping record. *"Shema Yisroel Adonai Elohaynu,"* I repeated, peeking out at the people cursing the downpour, passing dripping coats to the rabbi's wife. Aunt Ruth was carrying a big box wrapped in gold paper; Shelley and Ronnie, her kids, each held smaller boxes. Michelle came in looking miserable in a stiff new dress. Grandpa held forth like a proud papa, wearing a blue-and-gold yarmulke—identical to the one I'd been given—fixed to his white hair with a bobby pin.

After a while, Rabbi Shlimkin introduced me and asked everyone to be seated. Feeling queasy, I stepped out in front of the guests and stood behind a lectern trying not to focus too hard on the fifty damp, expectant faces. The next half hour passed in a panicked blur. Rabbi Shlimkin sat in the front row mouthing the words as I chanted my script; Mom nodded to my hurried rhythm as if she were hearing the bossa nova; Belle, who thought Hebrew sounded funny, giggled all the way through. I managed to stay on track somehow and not skip a single verse. When I'd finally finished the last section, Grandpa had puddles under his eyes. As people pushed toward me in the reception hall, he told me that I sang like an angel. "The boy should be a cantor, Eye."

My mother gave me a look that said *over my dead body.* "There's plenty of time to decide, Dad."

Grandpa blew his nose into a handkerchief and took his glasses off to dry his cheeks. He bent over to hold my face between his hands and kissed me on the lips in front of everyone. Then, with a flourish, an envelope appeared from his jacket pocket. "You'll take this and be very careful," he said, handing me the gift. "My grandson, the cantor," he said again.

"Thank you, Grandpa."

"Remember," he said. "It don't grow on trees."

For the next half hour, I walked around the reception hall, having my cheeks pinched and holding out the shoebox that Mom made me bring along for gifts, like a street urchin after a tap dance. Later at home, we sat on her bed and counted the loot—seven hundred dollars!—most of it in a savings bond from Grandpa. Sitting on the blanket with her, surrounded by checks with my name on them, I felt rich for the first time. I did not, however, feel like a man.

· twenty-six ·

What was a man supposed to feel like? This was the fathomless mystery. When it came to the workings of a man's heart, the instinct he'd have for finding the door and knowing how to enter the world—the things a woman can't teach a boy, no matter how hard she tries—I was completely stumped. How could I inhabit this skin, and ride this charging force inside that set me apart from the female world? There was no one around to explain what to do with this masculine power, which felt (like a bull in a china closet) too big, too loud, too fierce, too hard, too wild, too *much* in every single way. Though puberty was changing my body, growing me physically into a man, I still felt like an in-between thing that watched and wondered but never fit. I improvised the best I could, invented myself from bits and pieces of what I saw in the men around me, but the result was more like *papier-mâché* than the solid article.

In the absence of a man to talk to, I questioned my own face reflected in glass. The bathroom was my laboratory, the mirror a kind of microscope for scrutinizing this person I was. I used the cosmetics at my disposal to try and discard different faces, to discover at what point I stopped being me—whoever that was—and starting becoming someone else. Sometimes I was Genghis Khan, scowling and uni-browed, other times I turbaned my head and puckered my lips like Marilyn Monroe. It wasn't that I wanted to be a girl—I very actively did not—but I needed to explore everything. When my mother saw traces of rouge on my face, she screamed bloody murder and ordered my sisters to hide their makeup, till I found the stuff buried in their panty drawer. While I was there, I figured, I might as well try on a bra as well.

Scouring the library for guidance or clues, I discovered *Christine Jorgensen: A Personal Biography,* the story of the first man to have a sex-change operation, and devoured it, fascinated by the notion that a person could actually become what he felt he was inside, invent himself against any odds. If a man could have his dick cut off and end up with his face on the cover of a book, I thought, anything was possible. Even more appealing than Christine Jorgensen was *Myra Breckinridge.* I'll never forget reading the first lines of that paperback, which thrilled me even more than Madame Curie ignoring her tumors: "I am Myra Breckinridge whom no man will ever possess." The hairs on the back of my neck stood up as I read nonstop till the last explosive page. Gore Vidal became my god. This spoof about a man-turned-woman who rules the world *like a man* was as close to a vision of personal power as I'd found till then in my gender drift. I was hypnotized by Myra's butchness, her ballsy domination of men, especially

Rusty, the cowboy-cum-actor, whose sphincter the author likened to an autumn tea rose. Those indelible words, and the joy with which Myra deflowered her prey, riveted and scared me. When I interviewed Gore Vidal many years later over lunch at the Saturnia hot springs near Rome, I told him that that tea rose had changed my life forever. Looking bloated and rheumy-eyed, my old hero chuckled. "Myra would have been pleased," Vidal said.

And yet, I knew that emulating women, or quasi-women, was not the answer; I already felt like a freak. While I walked home from school one afternoon with my gang of weirdo friends, fey geeky boys and smart ugly girls that nobody else would talk to, a bunch of roughnecks surrounded us on their Sting Rays. They teased the girls without touching them, then beat the rest of us over the head with their books, and held our arms while they took turns kneeing us in the crotch. I broke away and ran as fast as I could, clutching between my legs. Staring into the bedroom dark that night, I made a—life changing, I hoped—decision, never to be that weak again. I swore that I'd make myself a man regardless of how it had to be done. I lay there underneath the blanket tensing my muscles till I was rigid, then vowed to myself through a clenched jaw that I would not become a sissy. I'd squeeze this girl part out of me, strangle her with pure will till I was all boy. I'd make myself strong and monochromatic, self-contained, one of *them*—if not in fact, then in appearance. I can still feel that moment's impact today, the determination to save myself, adapt to the world, not be a victim or a freak. I'd keep my backbone straight, head up, chest out, heart sewn up tight as a soldier's.

I threw out my book on Madame Curie and returned Myra Breckinridge to her shelf at the library. In the C volume of the encyclopedia, I came across a drawing of the Colossus of Rhodes straddling its island harbor, dwarfing everything at its feet. According to the blurb I copied, this huge, glistening, muscular statue was among the Seven Wonders of the World, a magnificent bronze monument to the sun god Helios that stood one hundred meters high. Although the Colossus was actually perched on a nearby hill, popular legend placed it alongside the harbor, forcing boats to pass between its legs. Now *here* was something to emulate, I thought, a golden giant who guarded the city, the entire Ancient World at its feet. I liked this idea of mythic power, and though the Colossus turned out to have been hollow, I didn't know this at the time. I knew only that I needed something oversized and luminous—a monumental symbol of strength—to transport me to the land of men.

· twenty-seven ·

"Hello, young man," said Joyce's friend, holding out his hand to me. He was fiftyish and oily-looking, with a beer belly popping out of his shirt and a ducktail dripping with Brylcreem. His teenage friend, blond and slim, tipped his chin at me.

"Hands off," said Joyce. "He's in junior high."

"I'll bet he is," Jerry, the fat man, said. The young man, Mark, gave me a wink.

Joyce had found them in a coffee shop in Hollywood. She was twenty-two, I was fourteen, and her husband Johnny had just hit the road. Three weeks after giving birth to their son, Brian, Joyce had gone to the baby's room for his morning feeding and found him cold and blue in his crib, dead from no apparent cause. She blamed herself and turned near catatonic; Johnny packed his bags and left. Emerging finally from her depression, lonely for company and eager for a non-stop party, she'd recently drifted into the gay scene, where loud fat girls were more than welcome.

They'd come over to swim in the pool next door and invited me to join them. Joyce and Jerry hid themselves in cutoffs and baggy T-shirts, while Mark stripped down to a chartreuse bikini with tiger paws appliquéd onto the hips. His chest was wide and hairless and flat, his arms and legs unusually muscled. He did jackknives off the diving board and swam underwater to where I was paddling, then tickled the bottoms of my feet. He came up sputtering with hair in his eyes.

"Race ya," he said and we took off fast, Joyce and Jerry rooting for us from their plastic chairs. Mark let me win by a length and toasted me with his Dr Pepper. Later when we went back to our apartment for showers, I lay down on Mom and Belle's bed, and when Mark came out of the bathroom, he dried himself in front of me, bending over to shake his hair and pat the towel under his arms.

"Good race," he said, pulling on his underwear. "You've got a good body for a swimmer."

"So do you," I said, trying not to sound like a fruit.

Mark and Jerry started showing up at our house whenever my mother wasn't home. Jerry had developed a crush on me, and though Joyce wasn't happy to share her friends, she liked how unexpectedly eager they were to spend more time with her. One day when she and Mark were outside and Jerry had gotten me all alone, I noticed that he was acting bashful.

"What's up?" I asked.

"You're a good kid," said Jerry.

"So?"

"Let's sit down." Jerry pulled out a chair at the kitchen table. "I've been wanting to talk to you," he said.

"What for?"

"You don't have a father," he said.

"Duh."

"I didn't have one, either." Jerry seemed uncomfortable. "I never had no one to talk to me."

"Anyone," I said. "Talk about what?"

He lit a cigarette and stared at me till I began to feel annoyed. "You probably don't know this," he finally said, "but you're a homosexual."

I felt as if I'd been slapped in the face. I'd never called myself *that* before. I'd never called myself anything. The groping I did in the neighborhood, the girls I made out with in the park or at the movies, the boys who beat off with me in their bedrooms in front of three-foot movie-star posters—Raquel Welch as a busty cavewoman, Brigitte Bardot leather-clad on a Harley, Norma Jean on red satin—and seeing whose semen could fly the farthest—all of this was just *messing around* undefined by clinical terms. In my naïve postpubescent mind, sex with boys was no different than with girls; it was something I did, not something I was. The H-word was oversized in the extreme, and all the more shocking when stuck to me by someone who'd unmasked me just by watching. In spite of my efforts to be nondescript, I'd been discovered by one of *them*, and feared what might be coming next: exile from the acceptable world, to the land of inverts and pansies and losers, men with prices on their flaming heads. Since this banishment mirrored how I already felt as a broken-home kid without a dad, the threat of being locked out and laughed at was all the more terrifying. Just as I wouldn't have chosen my family, I wouldn't have joined this creepy club either, or accepted the alien citizenship Jerry seemed to be handing me.

"I hope I didn't hurt your feelings."

"I am not a sissy," I said.

"I never said you were," Jerry answered. I snapped my hand back when he tried to touch it. Half of me wanted to punch him out. The other half wanted to bawl like a baby.

"I'm telling you this for your own good."

"Gee, thanks."

"You'll always remember this conversation. You'll probably even thank me someday."

"Don't hold your breath."

"There's nothing wrong with the way you are. No matter what you hear out there. Don't ever be ashamed of yourself. I'd give my eyeteeth to have known that at your age. But things were different in those days."

I was too confused to appreciate how hard Jerry was trying to help me. Instead, I acted like I'd been insulted and got out of there as soon as I could.

The valley was so hot that summer that people fried eggs on the sidewalk, birds plummeted dead from the trees, and mothers wore oven mitts to open their car doors at noon. Julie took my mother to his ski chalet at Lake Tahoe when his wife and children were away in Europe—he'd bought his own trucking company by then, and drove a shiny black Lincoln Town Car. Marcia had left the Valley with her psychotic first husband, who rarely allowed her to come home. It was just Mom and us by then, so Belle was left for me to take care of. We walked around in our underpants and ate cold food straight from the fridge. At night, we put blankets out on the grass and slept underneath the stars. By morning, the blankets were soaked through with dew.

On the afternoon that it finally happened, Joyce took Belle to a triple-feature to escape the heat, and I was left alone in the house. Though I'd barely said two words to Jerry since our talk, Mark and I were becoming friends. The fact that I was in junior high and he was five years older didn't seem to bother him. He assured me that Jerry had meant no harm and related the story of how they'd met, after Mark had run away from home: the older man had given him a place to stay. I came to trust Mark, so that after a while, when he told me that Jerry was taking him to the beach, and wondered if I wanted to join them, I said yes.

They picked me up in Jerry's convertible wearing matching baseball caps. Jerry had a cigar in his teeth and a Hawaiian shirt unbuttoned to his navel; Mark was shirtless and smoking a joint, which he passed to me as we sped through Topanga Canyon on our way to Santa Monica. I'd smoked pot only once before, with Rima Louise, and all it had done was give me a headache. Now, Mark showed me how to inhale, how to hold the smoke in my lungs, and soon my brain was tingling as the car took hairpin curves up the mountain, past hippies selling batik and candles, shacks with guard dogs and dirty-faced toddlers; past sagebrush fields, and electric red poppies that edged the canyon ridge like a garland, all of it bright and pulsatingly vivid. Mark was waving his arms and shouting, his golden hair, platinum blond at the temples, blown straight back from his face. He stood up in the car while Jerry held his leg, and yanked off a eucalyptus branch, then rubbed the silvery leaf in his palms and held his hands underneath my nose. I breathed the menthol off his skin, and when I looked up his green eyes were laughing.

We parked at Santa Monica. Mark heaved the ice chest onto his head—I took the radio—and we followed Jerry away from the pier till we came to a section of beach that was crowded with men in all directions, without a single female in sight. I'd never been in a gay place before, and walking through this amazing mosaic of sun-baked men in their colored swimsuits, laid side by side like multi-hued tiles, I felt dizzy from dope and heat and fear. Once we set up camp on our blanket, I stared dumbstruck at this strange new world, men hugging and holding hands in the open, playing chicken in the water. I watched them in groups of three, five, and more, interlocking limbs on their towels, rubbing lotion on each other's backs, shielding their eyes as they cruised the beach, or held books to their faces with Coppertoned fingers. On top of the lifeguard stand, a towheaded guy with white paste across his nose looked out at the water through mirrored shades, apparently unfazed by the scene. I lay in my trunks between Mark and Jerry, listening to *Suite: Judy Blue Eyes*, taking in every detail around me—a panorama of male shapes and sizes more varied than I had ever imagined—and after a while I began to relax. I started to think as the hours passed that if this was a slice of life among homos, this world might not be so grotesque after all. These men looked just like other men; even their shows of affection seemed normal, not so different from guys at school tackling each other after a game, or walking arm in arm through the halls.

There was a difference—I understood that—but it wasn't a difference that couldn't be hidden in places where it wasn't welcome, or revealed in others, like this, where it was. It thrilled me to realize, for the first time, that men who liked men were not condemned to inhabit a netherworld of slimy losers, or hide themselves fully from everyday life.

We swam, and ate, and smoked more joints, and when the sun began to set, we packed our things and walked back to the car, Mark's arm around my shoulders. Back in the Valley, they asked me if I wanted to stop off and take a shower at a nearby motel. I knew the Aladdin already from the purple matchbooks that Mom brought home some Wednesday mornings, a curly-toed genie sketched on the cover. Mark and I ducked down in the front seat while Jerry checked in. Inside the room, I sat by the window waiting tensely for their first move, watching the fan on the mirrored ceiling slowly turn over the king-sized bed. We took turns showering separately, and after Mark and I were finished, and Jerry had closed the bathroom door, the blond boy led me toward the bed. When Jerry came out, I lay between them feeling like a prince in a harem as they took turns stroking my hair, kneading my biceps, telling me how good I tasted. I watched our bodies moving in the frosted mirror overhead—Jerry's round and soft and white, Mark's ultra-lean and carefully muscled—and when we couldn't come anymore, I fell into a trancelike sleep and awoke with my face in the crook of Mark's arm. He looked like he was protecting me, his shoulder curved around my head, while Jerry snored on the other side. I felt in that moment completely at home, more comfortable than in my own bed. The sign clicked on in the parking lot and a neon genie flashed in the window, beaming colors across the bed. I watched my face go orange and blue, then normal again, as the lights around the sign flashed in sequence.

Technically, this was child molesting, but a happier molestation would be hard to imagine. Sadly, it never happened again—Jerry and Mark moved to San Francisco soon afterward—but they left me far more self-assured than when they found me. I'd learned the important though dangerous lesson, common to young men their first time out, that "grown-up" sex was the shortest distance between one's lonely, tormented self and the affirming touch of the rest of humanity. Though this shortcut would later get me in trouble, it at first seemed an excellent strategy. Enjoyable as sex was, however, especially at that rambunctious age, it was rarely my primary interest. I wanted male companionship, the affection of surrogate fathers and brothers, even more than I wanted men's bodies. Now and then in an embarrassing moment, my deeper motives escaped inadvertently: once after sex with someone I'd known for half an hour I blurted out *I love you* and sent the guy into mean gales of laughter. Mostly I kept my agenda secret and managed to play a less threatening role as unleashed teenage kid on the prowl, aware that under this horny guise I was actually someone else, looking for something these men couldn't give me. In time, I came to resent how little they knew about me besides my body, but figured at first—as Mom had, too, when discovering the power a body could wield—that it was better to be known in parts, and pursued for shallow, limited reasons, than not to be known at all.

· twenty-eight ·

Sullivan's been out of town for two weeks, and Liz has no new information about the suspect in California. Doctor G is equally out of touch. Though I'm in his treatment room twice a week, though he draws my blood monthly and studies my skin with a magnifying glass, he has no idea who I really am. In the months since I've been seeing him, he's never once asked me about my life, or what I do when I'm not in his office. He asks me about my symptoms (none), ticks off boxes in columns on charts, keeps a meticulous record of weight loss (none) and cell counts, but has no interest whatsoever in anything besides my body. This focus on my cells and numbers makes me feel I'm not quite human and, in his eyes, certainly doomed.

One day at Barbara's apartment, helping her with a piece she's writing, I'm hit by a panic attack so intense that I'm forced to lie down on the floor, while Barbara sits next to me holding my hand.

It's like being trapped on the Gravitron, the carnival ride where the wall spins and the floor drops and you're flattened against the wall like a bug with a pin through your neck, going faster and faster till everything blurs. Barbara tries to calm me down, but it's obvious she's as scared as I am. Finally we sit on her floor, my fingers clutching the fuzz of the carpet. She holds my hand and lets me cry.

I'm home alone when Aunt Ruth calls to say she's got a surprise for me. "I thought it was lost—oh, honey, you'll love this!" she says. It's been six months since Uncle Marty died, and she's only now worked up the nerve to empty out his drawers and closet. Behind fishing equipment and ping-pong-ball cans, she's come across something that I'll want to see.

"What is it?" I ask.

"I'm not telling."

"Give me a hint."

"No hints," she says.

"Aunt Ruth!"

"It's black and white."

"A movie?"

But she will not be inveigled. Underneath her marshmallow exterior, Aunt Ruth negotiates like a shark. She'll do almost anything to lure the family back from the diaspora. Ronnie has settled in San Diego, Shelley's spent several years in Israel on a kibbutz, "looking for herself," as she tells her mother. "At her age I didn't know I was lost," Aunt Ruth likes to say.

"A family movie?"

"Come and see. You'll be happy. I promise."

I fly to the west coast three days later. When the taxi pulls up to Aunt Ruth's house, she's waiting on the porch with outstretched arms. Several enormous black garbage bags are lined up on the front porch.

"What's that?" I ask.

"Uncle Marty," she says.

"I'll take them away."

"Later," she says. "First you'll come and see."

The projector is already set up in the living room, the draperies drawn. The room has been completely done over; in place of the gold vinyl sofa, I'm sitting now on peach chintz, matched by pastel-tinted wallpaper. Her *Fiddler on the Roof* village scenes of flying rabbis and twirling dancers have been replaced by gouache meadows and a van Gogh lithograph. All that remains from the old decor are the pictures of grandparents and great grandparents from the old country, hung in a gallery by the TV set—gaunt, intense, accusing faces with glowering eyes over stiff black clothes.

"I should have made some popcorn," says Aunt Ruth, threading the reel-to-reel. When she finally gets the contraption running, she flips off the lights, turns on the projector, and sits down next to me on the couch. Scratches blip across the screen, then a pair of hands hold up a bedsheet with SHELLEY'S FIFTH BIRTHDAY PARTY written across it in fancy lettering. Underneath is a child's rendition of the MGM lion roaring through its porthole. Grandpa appears on the screen after that with a mane of dark hair, lifting Shelley up and down for the camera, legs kicking, a party hat slipping off the side of her head. The camera swerves to a young woman in capris and a tie-up blouse, laying paper plates on a picnic table, waving the camera away and smiling.

"Your Uncle Marty drove me crazy with that stupid thing," Aunt Ruth says, watching her young self projected onscreen. "I can't believe I was ever that skinny, it makes me sick. Look, here comes Joycie."

A round-faced cherub with blond ringlets suddenly jumps into the frame, waving her arms like pinwheels. Behind her is a sad-eyed girl smiling shyly, picking at her bangs, waving at the camera. When the camera zooms in on Marcia's face, Aunt Ruth sighs and touches my hand.

The scene changes to the patio, where a bunch of kids run around in circles, playing games around twirling Shelley. The lens pans away from the children past the orange trees in Aunt Ruth's backyard, up to a bird on a telephone line and down to the picnic table, where an attractive young couple are leaning together. At first, I don't recognize my mother, wavy hair falling past her shoulders. She has her hand hooked on her companion's bicep; his shirt sleeves are rolled up like a workman's. He's talking to someone over his shoulder, then turns and smiles straight into the camera.

"Oh, my God," I say.

For the first time in my adult life, I'm looking at my father's face. I can't describe the sensation of this, or the jolt of wondering how I'd forgotten—or thought I'd forgotten—a face so immediately familiar. Our features are nearly identical—he's almost the same age I am now—and when he winks and cocks his head, thirty years seem to dissolve between us. I remember his face intimately, as if I'd seen him an hour ago, been knocked unconscious and woken up. Tracing the line of his neck with my eyes, where my mother's fingers are paused at the collar, I think to myself in bold type, HE'S REAL.

"I'll leave you alone," Aunt Ruth says, and after she's gone I freeze frame the film at the crest of his smile. Staring, I'm filled with a tirade of feelings—vindication, excitement, sadness, redemption, confusion, loneliness, rage; I sit there for the longest time, memorizing his face again, letting the *fact* of my father sink in. A few hours later, I leave the house with the film can packed inside my suitcase. It feels like having a piece of him with me, rare and precious evidence. At the airport, I call Belle and swear her to secrecy—I've never come to L.A. without visiting before, but she understands—and promise to send her a copy of the movie when I duplicate one for Sullivan. Then I call Mom before the plane leaves, pretending to be home in New York. She sounds a little hazy and weak, having slept through most of the day. "I was dreaming about you," she says.

· twenty-nine ·

After fourteen years of rendezvous, secret vacations, tormented phone calls, postcards from places like Athens and Cairo, signed only with hearts and an X; after offering to leave his now-bedridden wife (which my mother refused to permit); after breaking off the affair and then returning to her full of lust and promises not to be so stupid again, Julie finally left Mom for good. I came home from the ninth grade one day to find a used yellow Bel-Air—his going-away present—parked in the space where the T-Bird had been. Mom was in bed with the venetian blinds closed, stubbing cigarettes out in a juice glass. I could hardly see her face in the dark. She didn't leave the bedroom for several days other than to use the toilet, and refused to let us open the window. Belle and I brought her food on a tray. Aunt Ruth called on the telephone but Mom refused to speak to her. Emma came and sat on the bed, listening to Mom berate herself for being such a goddamn fool.

"You're loyal like a dog," Emma told her, but this only made my mother feel worse. I took the car keys out of her purse and beat off in the back seat of the Bel-Air, disgusted by the whole situation. Emma finally put her foot down and refused to go home unless this nonsense stopped. We watched my mother emerge from the dark room looking like a zombie and understood, without being told, that Julie's name must never be mentioned again.

Emma convinced Mom to get off welfare and go back to work. "Security, Ida," Emma said. "You need to stand on your own two feet. Enough with the men."

"You're not kidding."

"A woman needs her own two cents. You're an intelligent human being, you need to start giving yourself some credit. There's a big world out there."

My mother was smart, as we came to find out. After studying for the civil service exam—the first time she'd opened a book since cking her way through high school—she scored in the ninety-sixth percentile, which brought her a number of good job offers and boosted her self-esteem. Since money had been her nemesis for most of her adult life, my mother chose a job in the Paymaster's Office at City Hall, handing out checks. She had special charge, ironically, of garnishing the wages of deadbeat fathers; week after week, delinquent cops, firemen, mailmen, and others showed up at her counter with trumped-up excuses for why they'd left their wives high and dry, and Mom had the consummate pleasure of docking their money till they were paid up. In the twenty-five years she'd spend at that desk, she earned the fear and respect of these slackers. "No more phony-baloney," she'd tell them, dangling their checks between her two fingers, just out of reach. "One more time and you're out on your ass."

I date my life as a criminal to the summer of 1971, two months after my mother went back to work, one month after Bruce McCauley first showed up on our doorstep holding a bunch of wilted daisies in his liver-spotted hand. I've recently come to learn that the arrest statistics for fatherless boys are nearly five times the national average and that this destructive tendency of elderless young men applies to other species as well. Adolescent bull elephants, for example, tend to go berserk when their fathers (or other adult males) have been wiped out by hunters; the young bulls kill cattle and ransack villages, forcing locals to gun them down to protect themselves. Without any viable man to stop me, I was a teenage danger as well, both to myself and to those around me. From the first time that Bruce showed up on our doorstep to take my mother out for dinner, glaring at me with his cruel yellow eyes, I wanted to do him serious harm.

My mother had done her best to avoid him, but Bruce worked in the office next door and had hounded her since the day they'd met—loitering around the door, leaving roses on her desk, sitting near her in the cafeteria, lingering under a nearby palm tree while she waited for her car pool. Since Bruce worked in Employee Relations, he was able to infiltrate Mom's file and began to call after dinner like clockwork. At first she let me screen the calls, but I was so obnoxiously rude that she started grabbing the phone herself, and agreed soon enough to have dinner with this stalker. She was used to having a man in her life, and Bruce was eager if little else. The night my mother finally caved in, she hung up the phone and laughed. "Oy vey, is this a live one."

I told her she couldn't go out with the creep.

"What's the difference, I'll eat dinner."

"He sounds like a pervert."

"Wait till you see him."

It was worse than Belle and I had expected, much worse. Bruce McCauley was hideous, with a Popeye chin, white-orange hair oiled flat on his skull, narrow mean tobacco-stained eyes, no visible lips, and grayish, too-small dentures that gave him a vicious look when he smiled, as he did, holding out his withered bouquet, when I opened the door. He was dressed in a turquoise blue polyester jumpsuit—short sleeves, attached belt—and white patent leather loafers. He held out his free hand, breathing booze fumes into my face. "You must be Ida's boy," he said.

"I'm her *son*," I answered, trying not to squeeze his hand.

"Shake it like you mean it," he said in an attempt to be cordial. He gripped my palm tight. "Feel that? That's how a man shakes. And you must be the little sister?"

Belle glared at the tipsy intruder from her place in front of the TV set. My mother emerged from the bedroom wearing lipstick, earrings, and high heels. "So I see you've met the kids."

"We're just getting acquainted," said Bruce. "I was just showing Junior here how to shake hands."

"Junior?" I asked. "Junior to whom?"

"I won't be late," Mom said quickly, bending down so that Belle could kiss her cheek, giving me a loaded look. Then they were out the door.

Clearly, I had to do something fast, stop this courtship before it went further and Mom messed up her life again. But Bruce was a formidable opponent. At sixty-eight, and thrice divorced, he claimed to want *security*, a concept more seductive to my mother at forty-four than anything to do with sex. He plied her with gifts and promises of everlasting devotion. We pleaded with her to play the field, not only because we didn't like Bruce, but because these few months were the first time we'd had her all to ourselves, when some man wasn't hogging her affection. But she couldn't help stringing Bruce along, claiming it made her feel like a woman to have a man so crazy about her.

"It's good for my ego," my mother said. I realized I couldn't compete with that.

"But you deserve someone better," I said.

"Since when? You think I'm so hot?"

"Someone nice will come along."

"Dream on, Gunga Din."

Bruce and I detested each other. From our very first contact, the animosity between us only grew more poisonous. As those months of courtship went by, I watched him assume more control of my mother. She worried about his opinions of things, waited around for Bruce to call. Soon, she was allowing this stranger to worm his way into our daily lives and to criticize how she was raising us. When I said something smart-alecky, he told her I needed *a good hard whipping upside the arse*, and Mom didn't disagree, fed up as she was with my big mouth. Bruce told my mother she deserved to be treated like a queen and, just to prove it, took her for a makeover at Max Factor's boutique off Hollywood Boulevard. Mom walked into the house that night looking like she'd been to a mortician, black hair under a bronzed dynel wig, cement-colored pancake makeup laid on with a trowel, scarlet rouge, hot-pink lipstick, painted eyebrows so severe Joan Crawford would have gone for the cold cream. She stood there in the doorway, hand on her hip, batting her false eyelashes. "Oh no," I said.

"Doesn't she look like a movie star?" asked Bruce, standing next to her in one of his pastel leisure suits.

She looked like a hooker on Medicare.

"Please don't be nasty," my mother said.

"But . . ." I stopped myself. I didn't want to hurt her feelings. Yet something had to be done right away.

The only question was what. I wanted to destroy Bruce Mc-Cauley, do him terrible bodily harm, but short of pouring Drano into his gin, I realized that this was impossible. I was no match for him physically—though he was old, his tattooed forearms were enormous—and while I'd have liked to duke it out, I needed to use my head to destroy him, to find his tender spot and strike. I feared what would happen otherwise; were my mother to marry this moron and bring him home as my stepdad, I'd have no choice but to run away, leaving Belle behind to suffer.

His automobile was the obvious answer. By then, Bruce was leaving his pride and joy, a brand-new, mint-green Cutlass Supreme, parked in our garage so that he could ride in Mom's car-pool. It wasn't hard to fish her spare set of keys from her purse, and wait for the right moment. Looking back from where I'm now sitting, I can't imagine why I believed I could get away with "grand theft auto" at fourteen with no experience behind a wheel, but consequences never crossed my mind. I was too deluded by vengeance, too convinced that Mom needed protecting, and that right was on my side, to entertain the notion of failure. On the morning that I played hooky, slipping the key into Bruce's ignition, I didn't see how I could fail at what seemed to me such a righteous crusade.

I didn't plan to smash up the car, or maybe I did without knowing it. I wanted to invade Bruce's turf as he had invaded mine, and perhaps leave some clue that he should get lost. I'd been watching how Mom drove for weeks and the moves seemed easy enough; indeed, after easing the car from the curb and steering myself onto a side street, driving seemed like a breeze at first. I'd stolen a pack of Mom's cigarettes and lit up in the car, breaking Bruce's cardinal rule against tobacco in automobiles, and made sure to flick the ashes onto the carpet and leave the stinking butts in the tray. I took the hula-girl deodorizer off the rearview mirror and broke off her head. At the end of the sidestreet, I waited till the coast was clear and turned onto the main boulevard. Then, since this was going so well, I decided to pull into a drive-through joint for some greasy food to leave on the seat. With french fries in hand, and a Coke oozing onto the Naugahyde dashboard, I was feeling extra fine when I turned the car out of the drive-through line and into the lane for oncoming traffic. Had I braked, no collision would have occurred; as it was, I hit the gas, jumped onto the curb, and rammed Bruce's Cutlass into the side of a large black Mercedes-Benz.

My head hit the windshield but I wasn't hurt. I sat there shocked in the driver's seat, drenched with soda, unsure about what to do next. *Run,* I thought, *get out of here,* but before I could even unbuckle my seat belt, sirens were screaming nearby and people were banging on the window. The cops who arrived in short order frisked me for a driver's license, realized I was too young to have one, and put me in the back seat of the squad car while they ran a check on Bruce's plates. The owner of the Mercedes sneered at me with crossed arms.

I refused to give the cops Mom's number at work. "You want to go to juvie?" they asked. I wanted to explain to them that this wasn't what it looked like at all. I wasn't a thief, not really, or some idiotic kid on a joyride. I was a good student, a reader of books, a decent young man trying to put a wrong thing right. I was running interference, like Telemachus with his mother's suitors while Odysseus was off somewhere drinking ouzo with the nymphs. But the cops, I knew, would never believe me. Finally, I gave them the number at City Hall, and when Mom showed up a half hour later, holding Bruce's arm in the taxi, I knew that it was all over for me. He was in, I was out; he had the sympathy, I was the bad guy. Bruce looked homicidal as he fingered the mangled fender and hood, wiped soda off the sticky dashboard, scooped the soggy tub of fries off the velour upholstery, searched underneath the seat for the missing, elm-scented hula girl. Mom turned her back to me, leaning against the hood of the cop car, the side of her mouth twitching madly. I wanted to tell her that I'd done this for her, but that would have sounded ridiculous.

Though the cops wanted to take me to jail, suggesting a night there would teach me a lesson, Bruce agreed not to press charges for my mother's sake. He reassured the Mercedes woman that his insurance would cover her damages, and we waited together for a tow truck. When I tried to apologize, Mom wouldn't listen; instead, to hurt me, she took Bruce's hand and said she'd make it up to him somehow. When the cars were finally taken away, the two of them walked home alone together without a glance back to see where I was.

I knew that I'd lost her for good this time and would never be able to win her back. In years to come the hatred between me and Bruce would range from simple vicious silence to his grabbing me by the throat on a bad drunk and threatening to punch me in the face. Afterward, I wanted to kill him. Instead, at fourteen, I withdrew from the race and replaced it with crime, sex, and narcotized madness.

·thirty·

"I've opened a big can of worms here," I say.

"Big worms, big fish," Joe replies in his office after lunch. His desk is piled high with manuscripts, memos, contact sheets, invitations, layout boards, and piles of old messages clipped together like dollar bills—the detritus of an editor's life. Whenever I come here I get the jitters like someone who's done time in Sing Sing. For three years, sixty hours a week, I labored at a similar job, trying to please an unpleasable boss, who hovered ghostlike in the background, lobbing complaints through his bad cops, grumbling behind his frosty mask, never once saying *good work* or *thank you*. But while he may have been a worse boss than most, Andy Warhol was far from unique. Most offices I know mimic bad families, with power-crazed parents crushing rebellion and angry kids sniping behind their backs. In the ten years since I'd walked out of my job, I'd never once regretted my choice.

Though I sometimes missed the paycheck, I never missed the sub-
jugation, the fretting over my spot on the ladder, the panting for
the master's approval. Joe tells me he envies my freedom—*golden
handcuffs*, he calls the job—but he isn't quite ready to leave the
game yet.

"I didn't think I'd remember so much," I say, as he sorts
through piles of mail.

"That's good," he says. "To remember is good."

"It's overwhelming," I say.

"Overwhelming is good."

Joe isn't listening. When his secretary buzzes to announce
calls on three separate lines, he kisses my hand and turns to the
phone. "Keep the faith," he says as I leave him to his afternoon.

At home, my desk is like an excavation site. I've started clip-
ping stories about fathers and sons from magazines and newspa-
pers. I've begun to read books along the same lines, a whole range
of filial lit that's never interested me before. Next to Sullivan's files
is a box of journals I haven't looked at since I first wrote them,
from elementary school till college. I feel lately as if I'm the second
detective here, pursuing my suspect backward in time, searching
for something I can't put my hands on. I'm not quite sure what
this hunted thing is, but a fairy tale I came across recently seems
to offer a kind of clue. In the story, an eight-year-old boy loses a
golden ball described by the author as "a radiance, a sense of unity
with the universe, wholeness, like the sun." It sounds farfetched to
describe my goal in these terms, whether I find my father or not.
Still, the image of lost wholeness moves me.

Next to the books of Freud, Jung, and Bly—and an excerpt of

Mitscherlich's *Society Without the Father*—I've gathered a collection of quotes to remind me that I'm not alone in this quandary surrounding the link between father and self. Among them are these imploring lines from a poem by Stanley Kunitz:

> *I called out to him to pay some attention to me*
> *To give me counsel on the conduct of my life.*
> *Father! I cried. "Return! You know the way,*
> *Instruct your son, whirling between two wars . . .*
> *Oh teach me how to work and keep me kind."*

Close by is perhaps my favorite quotation, from psychologist Rollo May, which sums up what I hope might result from capturing the mythic golden ball:

> What is this experience (of wholeness) like? It is like the experience of the poets of the intuitive world, the mystics, except that instead of pure feeling of and union with God, it is the finding and union with my own being. It is like a child in grammar school finding the subject of the verb in a sentence—in this case the subject being one's own life. It is ceasing to feel like a theory toward one's self.

And scattered others as well:

> "For the first time since childhood, men in their late thirties experience the need to reconnect with their fathers." (Robert Bly)

"Our lives may be determined less by our childhoods than by the way we have learned to imagine our child-hoods." (James Hillman)

"Does any man know who his father is?" (Homer)

"At the moment of clasping [his father], Telemachus comes of age." (Stanley Kunitz)

"Loving, he waded down into more ancient blood, to ravines where horror lay, still glutted with his fathers." (Rainer Rilke)

"It's a father's day and everybody's wounded." (Leonard Cohen)

More than what I'm learning in books, I'm struck by the personal stories coming to me now from all directions. My newfound father-antenna is picking up the daddy channel everywhere I turn. People I've known for years are sharing their father secrets with me for the first time. Hearing them, I'm struck by two things: that nearly everyone I talk to seems to share this father hunger, and that without exception these same people are spiritual seekers. Without equating these distinct paths, it's impossible to deny the connection, as I realize while talking to Gary.

"My father died when I was five," he tells me over coffee. We're writing buddies—Gary's a playwright—and when he hears about Mac Sullivan, this talented guy turns on like a faucet. Gary looks like an Irish boxer with his shaven head, jug ears, and bone-crushing arms, but as he talks about his father, he resembles more clearly a teary-eyed boy.

"I remember running down the street after the hearse to stop them from taking him away," Gary tells me, "I never stopped running after that. I was always searching for someone to find me. I had this God-sized hole in my chest."

Right, I think. A God-sized hole.

"I could never fill the hole up. Nothing would stay long, since I wasn't solid. I wasn't *real*. I had no idea about who I was 'cause nobody ever told me. I was always inventing myself. That must be why I write plays. I'm still trying to figure out how you can make a character true. How you can make up an authentic life."

"What about relationships?" I ask.

"I'm always waiting for them to leave me. I never think they're telling me the truth. When they say they love me, I wonder *who* they think they're loving, even if I care for them. I'm always performing in one way or other, trying to act like a big man."

"How does a big man act?"

"Macho. Possessive. Promiscuous. Stupid. I just want to feel like *somebody*. I want to feel like I'm living *my life*. Not like some kid running down the street chasing his father's hearse. I'm thirty-four years old, for Chrissake."

"So what do you do?"

"I pray," says Gary. "I pray to stop running. I pray to stay sober. I pray to learn how to be a man—a real man, not a macho asshole. I pray to believe I deserve to be here and that someone could love me for who I am. Not for my brain or my dick or my money. *Me*. And that I could like who I really am, too. That's what I pray for every day, but I'm not there yet."

"We live in a fatherless culture," says Martha, a therapist acquaintance who invites me over when she hears about Mac Sullivan. The room hasn't changed in over a decade: the same oatmeal-colored furniture, macramé wall hangings, wandering Jews hanging limp in their pots. Martha hasn't changed either, soft-spoken, curly-haired, dressed in her usual kibbutz chic. She pours herself a cup of tea and kicks back the legs of her Barcalounger.

"Most of my clients have deep father hunger, physical, emotional, or spiritual. There's a deep longing for male protection. A hunger for real masculinity. On a primitive, child's level."

"What do you mean by real?" I ask.

"Not invented. Men with that kind of self-belief aren't fragmented in quite the same way—their maleness doesn't come crashing down every time it isn't stroked. Macho men invent themselves from an idea. It's really an act of what a man should be. There's a major difference between real masculinity, real fathering, and what most of us get. If you don't have the real thing, then you can't be a father to your son, and the wheel goes round and round."

"Half-men," I say.

"Half-people," says Martha. "Women need fathers, too. The truth is this culture's in big trouble. Until we have more real fathers around, and women who allow them to be fathers, we're going to be split. I see big tough men nearly every day, fathers themselves, fall apart when they talk about this, sitting right where you are now. I see amazing men who have everything—looks, money, culture, brains—whose lives go nowhere because there was no man around who said, 'You're good, be successful, I believe in you, you matter. I give you my blessing. Have a great life.'"

"You make it sound so simple," I said.

"Not so simple. But possible."

"Even after the fact?"

"It doesn't matter when it happens. But the connection has to be made."

"What if I don't find him?" I ask.

"Then you'll bury him," Martha tells me, "and that in itself will be a blessing." When the next patient rings the doorbell, Martha stands up to hug me. The top of her head comes up to my chin. "I'll help you throw the dirt," she says.

· thirty-one ·

Fourteen to seventeen are blurred together, claustrophobic teen-age years propelled by hormones, rage, revenge, and all the drugs I could find. With my mother at work and Bruce in the background—telling her I was a big boy now who needed to learn from my own hard knocks—I spun completely out of control. This was L.A. in the Seventies, when a decent-looking kid craving trouble could open any number of doors, day or night, and lose himself for as long as he wanted. Meeting people wasn't hard; I stuck out my thumb and they appeared: men, women, kids my age. Eighteen months after my bar mitzvah, my nerdy life had transformed itself into a psychedelic satyricon of musical beds and lost weekends, handfuls of pot, Quaaludes, hash, speed, MDA, mescaline, magic mushrooms, THC, cocaine, opium, and liquid acid dropped in my eyeballs. I put a lock on my bedroom door and covered the walls with obscene graffiti; eventually, I stopped going to school except at exam time, when I stumbled in hung over, bug-eyed, contemptuous. The first time I was arrested, just after my fifteenth birthday, a cop handcuffed me in history class after getting a tip on my gym-locker pharmacy. My classmates watched as he led me to his squad car, and didn't see me again for the rest of the year, after I was transferred to another district.

I wanted to die, but I didn't know it. All I knew was I had to get out—out of the suburbs, away from my mother, out of the craziness brewing inside me. As long as I was high and gone, I didn't care where I disappeared to; there was no place that I could fit anyway. This manic, three-year, drug-addled fiasco terrified the people around me. Mom had no idea how to stop me; she chewed her nails, bailed me out of jail, kept food on the table, looked the other way. Belle was scared I'd leave one night and turn up in a ditch somewhere. Bruce concluded that I was a bad seed, and that this was what came of sparing the rod. Finally, her nerves in shreds, my mother told him to shut his big mouth or get the hell out and not come back.

The situation came to a climax the third time I was thrown in jail. When Mom saw me stumble out of the cell, shortly after my seventeenth birthday, she looked as if she was going to faint. I was barefoot in overalls with no shirt underneath, hair Ajaxed platinum blond, face caked with blood from where the cops had hit me, and cuts on both wrists from the handcuffs. I saw her face through a Quaalude haze, and when I smiled, the scab on my lip where the cops had beaten me split apart and bled profusely. After finding me with my head through the windshield—I'd totaled two parked cars—the officer had asked for my license, but instead of cooperating, I'd grabbed him by the collar and yanked him against the driver's door. The next thing I knew, I was in a chair with my cuffed hands looped around the back, getting pushed over backwards and crashing down on my elbows.

Now, Mom was looking at me horrified, clutching her purse, mouth open. "You're gonna end up in Alcatraz," she said.

· thirty-two ·

I knew she was right but I couldn't stop. I needed someone to sit hard on me, pin me down till I could see straight. I needed someone stronger than I was to help break this thing that wanted to kill me. This was only a vague awareness in me, glimpsed through a veil of narcotic commotion. Yet even in my most twisted moments, I guarded the hope that I could be saved—helped to save myself from myself—by someone I needed to think might be out there. Whether this faith was a dream wish or not, it gave me strength in a pitch-dark time—as the faith in an unseen Savior can—and may even have helped me to stay alive.

A few months after my last arrest, my luck began to turn around. One summer night around two A.M., I was loitering near the pool table in the only gay bar in Palm Springs when I saw a strange-looking man glaring at me through the cigarette smoke.

His thumbs were hooked into his hip pockets, and the curly hair falling out of his ski cap made him look like Wild Bill Hickok. He wore a flannel shirt unbuttoned to the ribs, a razor-thin beard, aviator glasses, and a strange gnarled black ornament that looked like a monkey's hand on a chain around his neck. I tried to return his stare but could hardly focus. Sloe gin fizzes go down like milkshakes, and I'd had more than I could count.

Bob LeMond ambled across the room and asked if he could buy me a drink. This is his version; mine is a blur.

"I look like I need a drink?" I asked.

"What is that? Tapioca?"

"Sloe gin. Extra shot."

"Don't move," Bob said, guiding me to a stool by the wall. When he came back with my cocktail, I didn't notice he'd left the booze out, and sucked the sweet stuff up through a straw. Five minutes later, we were in his car.

"Where we going?" I asked, head hanging out the window, as we sped up Highway 117 into the desert, a hot wind blowing through my surfer shag. "Arizona?"

"Trust me," said Bob.

"Yeah, right."

At the sign for the Morongo Indian Reservation, we turned off the highway and did a limbo under the barbed-wire fence. The desert was bleached a ghostly white, with a brilliant full moon overhead. I followed the reflection off Bob's silver-studded belt toward the foot of the mountains, past tumbleweeds and piles of quartzite glowing in burned-out campfire circles. After what seemed like an hour's walk, we came to a huge flat-topped boulder, climbed on top of it, and took off our clothes. I stood on the edge, pounded my chest, and yodeled into the wild like Tarzan.

A few hours later, I opened my eyes to the sight of the sun's first glow over the Mojave, and the feeling of Bob covering my cold body with a towel. At the touch of his arm in that protective gesture, I thought with vivid clarity *love*.

That week, I packed my things and moved into Bob's bungalow in the Hollywood Hills. We didn't discuss this happening, nor did I ask my mother's permission. I threw some clothes into a duffel bag, piled my journals and books in a box, and left a note stuck to the fridge, telling Mom and Belle that I'd be in touch. On our second night together, Bob had turned to me in bed—crooked teeth, crinkly eyes—and said in his Texas twang, "You're a mess but you've got potential." That was all I needed to hear.

He was old enough to be my father, with twenty-one years between us exactly, and the bossiest person I'd ever met. He was also smart and very funny, honey-tongued as an old cowboy. As a personal manager, Bob was paid to control people's lives: actors came from around the country to put themselves in his expert hands, like unfinished statues swarming around Pygmalion. In those first weeks after I'd moved in, I eavesdropped on him speaking to prospective clients. His authority awed me—Bob could spend ten minutes talking to a stranger, then dissect him down to his last neurosis, lay out his strengths and weaknesses, and outline a game plan for his success. In the five years that we were together, I watched him turn bar bouncers into movie stars, chorus boys into daytime TV heartthrobs, and turkey-necked Broadway has-beens into tucked, dyed, wisecracking mothers earning twenty-five thousand dollars a week on prime-time sitcoms. Bob's formula for success was simple: use what you've got to get what you want.

I took this at first as the gospel truth, and, eager to be successful myself, I turned myself over to Bob's expert hands. "Remember one thing," he said, paraphrasing Oscar Wilde. "Only superficial people do not believe in appearances." Bob treated me to cowboy boots like the ones he wore, a turquoise belt, silk shirts, new blue jeans, and the first suit I'd ever owned, navy blue with pleated cuffs and a hole for a boutonniere. He got me a decent haircut, drilled me on saying *pardon* instead of *huh*, demonstrated how not to slurp my spaghetti in public *(twirl it in the spoon, darlin', that's what it's there for),* corrected my posture *(you're hunched over like you're starving!),* schooled me in how to appear conversational at industry parties when I was tongue-tied (nearly always), showed me the proper way to fold my underwear, to walk without dragging my feet, to shave without leaving razor burn; and taught me, sitting next to him at the piano, why Elgar was greater than Purcell could ever hope to be. In exchange for his generosity, I gave Bob the only things I had—a starving mind to feed as he pleased, devotion bordering on idolatry, a body to help build (and play with), a character to construct, and a new protégé to show off to his circle of admiring friends.

Described in this way, our relationship sounds sordid—exploitive, unequal, an awful cliché—like the stories of kept boys and men who control them, each side sucking the other dry in vampirical *arrangements* of stand-in daddies and whorish sons. But that was not the case at all. Bob and I had good times together and made an excellent team; our life at first was symbiotic, and even later when I rebelled and the chemistry grew more explosive between us, we remained legitimate, passionate lovers, as satisfied with each other as any so-called equal partners. The power I gave him was freely given; I may have been desperate, but I wasn't stupid. I realized that I could learn more from Bob in a week, about being a man and making my way in the world, than I had in a lifetime from anyone else.

The skill I envied most of all, the gift that truly boggled my mind, was Bob's capacity to be happy. He leapt out of bed most mornings like a kid with a boxful of presents, ready for the day to surprise him. Such *joie de vivre* was absolutely novel to me—especially in a successful man—a jolt of positive energy that rendered getting high unnecessary (even if Bob hadn't frowned on it). Every morning just after dawn, we put on our shorts and running shoes and jogged up into the hills near our house, past tile-roofed mansions with wrought-iron gates, stucco walls splashed with bougainvillea, past low-hanging poplars and eucalyptus that turned the air fantastically fresh. I'd watch Bob ahead of me, always a few steps ahead, his short, well-muscled legs moving steadily, fists clenched, chin down, wide shoulders swinging, and let myself fall into his rhythm. At the top of the hill where the houses ended, we'd stop to catch our breath, the quiet city laid out before us. I'd study Bob's sweaty face from the side, beard and mustache marbled with gray, and think that there was nowhere on earth I'd rather be than standing right behind him, gearing up for another big day.

I thrived on the discipline Bob encouraged, and felt, for the first time, almost worthy, almost a player, almost a man. The fierce ambition I'd hidden since boyhood, silenced with dope, swallowed in time as sour grapes—the intensity I'd found so overwhelming—quickly began to uncurl itself. Though I didn't covet his show-business life, I was greedy for success of a different kind, a writer's success, which, after reading a story I'd written, Bob promised me I could have someday if I was willing to work like a dog. I threw myself into books again, Kafka, Hesse, Genet, Woolf, Forster, Flaubert, Miller, Gide, any author who caught my eye in our neighborhood bookstore. At my high-school graduation, Bob sat with Mom, Belle, and Marcia, charming them all with his Hollywood tales. Though my mother didn't know quite what to make of our friendship—when I'd tried to explain the ins and outs, she'd said, *I don't want to hear about it!*—she seemed grateful that Bob was helping me. I was coming home clean and sober now, well dressed, with stories about the famous people I was meeting, the classes I was planning to take at Los Angeles City College, my job at the local health-food store. However much she might have wished that Bob was more like a Jewish Big Brother and less like her hairdresser Pepe, she gave us her unspoken blessing.

Our troubles began in the fall of 1975, after eighteen months of living together and two unexpected changes of fortune. First, a favorite client of Bob's, a blue-eyed boy he'd discovered in a high school musical, hit it big in a TV series, and soon after in a disco film that turned him into a superstar, moving Bob from the B-plus to the A list of Hollywood machers. Second, I realized that Bob wasn't perfect; in fact, I was as smart as he was. There's no one on earth more condescending than a nineteen-year-old wannabe writer, and after I'd started at L.A.C.C., with photos of Tolstoy and Proust on my desk, Bob's values began to appear adolescent next to the high-minded views of my icons. His insistence on pleasure at all costs, however ostentatious, seemed silly and increasingly vapid. With the megalithic success of his client, we'd moved in the space of a few months from our modest two-bedroom bungalow to a sprawling ranch house with manicured lawns and a hot tub. There were Lear jets now, and limousines, poolside cabanas at famous hotels, late-night screenings with studio heads, a huge black Mercedes in the driveway, an eight-line telephone, hair plugs to cover Bob's galloping baldness, pedicures, weekly shopping binges, a staffload of flunkies running to buy him breath mints. Next to our bedroom were three walk-in closets lined from floor to ceiling with dry-cleaning bags, thirty pairs of cowboy boots, belts made of skins stripped from endangered species, accordion rows of perfect pleats. As Bob's ego and bank account exploded, his confidence began to seem shrill, his obsession with image and status vulgar—*unmanly*, in fact—at least for the man that I wanted to be.

I judged him harshly and selfishly, like a child who realizes one sad day that his parents are flawed humans rather than gods. Though I realized how much he'd done for me, my hero worship of Bob was over, and his fall from the pedestal came with a crash. While I loved him as much as a young man can love, who's barely begun to know himself, it had always been his serious side—the Bob who liked to play the piano, read in the garden, talk about paintings in the museum—that truly attracted me. It seemed to me now that he'd pawned off those parts for cultured status, reputation, and flash. "Can't you just lighten up?" he'd beg me, stomping his feet when I got moody, complaining that I was ruining his *fun*—a word I'd increasingly grown to despise as Bob's obsession with playthings increased. His refusal to admit that he was wrong or to entertain opposing viewpoints—mine, for example, which I voiced with increasing petulance—his obsessive need to shape and control me (as well as everyone else around him), the rigid self-certainty I'd equated with strength and now saw as a form of smallness, were becoming impossible to live with, and by the end of our second year, although I was far too scared to leave him, the tension between us was close to deadly.

Bob had become a servant to fame, his wagon hitched to his star client. Next to our bed was a special phone that rang around the clock, waking us whenever his boy wonder needed a stroke, or advice, or a friend. Listening to Bob in the dark as he soothed, flattered, and coddled the actor, I felt betrayed and jealous, pushed aside as the number-one son, although I never said so. Instead, I turned stubborn and sullen; we could hardly speak without fighting, locking horns over every trivial thing. Neither of us would back down—I'd learned Bob's martial lessons too well for that. Emotionally speaking, his house grew too small for both of us.

I wanted to go to a better school, and Bob—hoping to cool the war without losing me (and clear some *fun* time for himself)—encouraged me to apply to Berkeley. I'd worked hard at City College, my grades were good, and the prospect of going away to a university excited me, even though it might be lonely. When a letter arrived offering me a full scholarship, I was elated at first, then panicked by the thought of moving out on my own. I took Bob's reassurance as a veiled desire to get rid of me, even though I was the one who was leaving. Today, of course, I understand my paranoia, but at the time it made no sense to me. Strangely, in all our years together, Bob and I never discussed my father or the effect of his disappearance on the genesis of our affair. He simply told me that the time had come for the two of us to grow apart if we hoped to stay together; that till I tested my own wings, I'd fight him for seeming to hold me back. I knew he was right and prepared to move out, with plans to come home every weekend. Before the plane landed in San Francisco, I already missed him.

Berkeley was a magical place, the campus self-enclosed and swarming with students from all over the world. Each morning, I walked down the hill from the room I rented in a redwood-shaded house with a view of the bay, through the early morning fog past the many-tiered rose garden, to the seminary where I ate my breakfast—eavesdropping on gay priests' adventures in the Castro—then into the campus itself. I passed the grand, neo classical library and made my way to the esplanade in front of Sproul Hall, past the lunatic we called the Hate Man, who stood knee-deep in the fountain, dressed in a lady's housedress and pearls, his beard matted, his scraggly hair braided like Pocahontas's, screaming *I HATE YOUR FUCKING GUTS!* to everyone who passed by. Then on through Sather Gate to Telegraph Avenue, and a table in the corner of the Cafe Med, where I liked to drink coffee and scribble.

I fell in love with Berkeley that autumn—the intellectual buzz of the place, the poets selling their work for a dollar, and found that as this love affair strengthened, alongside a newfound need for solitude, my attachment to Bob began to change.

Though we spoke every night on the telephone, and I left every Friday afternoon for the forty-minute flight to L.A., our time together was growing more awkward. At home, our intimacy was strained. The more I matured, the less we connected; the larger I grew in ideas and self-image, the less I could wedge myself into the boy role that being with this man demanded. Knowing this saddened our time together, but coming back on Sunday afternoons to my single bed with the carved headboard, my typewriter, books, and basement hotplate glazed with fried spaghetti sauce, the pine trees outside my window and the bay glittering in the distance, I felt so free that the sadness soon faded, and my other life seemed far away.

When Bob made it clear to me that long-distance monogamy wasn't an option, I began simultaneous love affairs with two of my professors. One Friday evening after French class, Laura, a voluptuous Breton fifteen years older, invited me to her bachelorette pad for couscous and some postprandial petting. Not long afterward, Mark, my ostensibly straight, unnervingly handsome Italian teacher, asked me to go to the movies and showed up at my front door with a box of chocolates, hurling me headlong into unrequited romantic hell. On my twenty-first birthday, Bob came north and threw me a party at a posh hotel in San Francisco, dominating the room as always, keeping my new friends (and, unbeknownst to him, beloveds) amused with his nonstop jokes and Texas charm. When I graduated Phi Beta Kappa and came home wearing a society ring, Bob puffed himself up as if I were his son. Two weeks later, he put me on a plane to Europe (we'd split the fare at my insistence) with the plan that Bob would join me later, after I'd spent time with Laura and Mark, both of whom were spending their vacations on the continent as well.

After two passionate months abroad, living with Laura on her farm in Andalusia, having my heart broken by Mark in Rome, where he finally kissed me drunkenly one night, then turned on me like an enemy, I met Bob in Florence. We spent three days walking the cobblestone streets, eating gelati, marveling at the squash-colored buildings, the lazy carp at the base of the Ponte Vecchio. We walked around the statue of David, whose tormented expression completely surprised me, then stood for a long time in the next gallery in front of Michelangelo's "Prigioneri," those eerie figures clawing themselves out of blocks of marble, hands and feet and sinewy shoulders clearing the rocks in which they're imprisoned. Bob said that these were his favorite statues and explained Michelangelo's theory that the figures he sculpted already existed inside the stone; his job as an artist, he believed, being simply to free them from their confinement.

I realized that Bob saw himself that way, too, drawing out the potential in the people who hired him for his magic touch. Yet there was only so much that a sculptor could do; there came a time when the figure had to step away from the hand that helped form it. As we stood there in the gallery together, sun coming in through the atrium window, I knew that I had reached that point, and that my time with Bob was over. I saw him off in Rome the next day, and when I returned to L.A. that fall, I moved what remained of my things from his house into a tiny studio near UCLA, where I lived during graduate school, and set my mind toward getting published. We spoke every few weeks and slept together one more time, colliding like sex-crazed maniacs after a drought one thundery night when I'd come for a visit. Afterward, we hugged at the door, and I felt, for a second, that Bob didn't want to let me go. Then he did, and made a joke—a hooker joke about no more freebies, and next time I'd have to buy him a drink—and opened the door for me to run through the rain to the car. Lightning had struck a tree next door; I could barely see through the windshield to steer around it as I drove away, not knowing what had passed between us. I would not know for another ten years, long after Bob had already died, and a nurse in a clinic delivered the news. I felt certain this virus had come from Bob, and after the initial panic had passed, realized—in lucid, philosophical moments—how appropriate it was that this man who'd helped me save my life, and been a kind of father to me, should have included this final gift, too—the harshest gift—to wake me up, as boys are awakened through tests of courage, tastes of death, emerging as men on the other side.

· thirty-three ·

It's a dark, wind-ripping morning. Louis and I wake up to the sound of metal crashing past our window onto the rooftop next door, close to the totemic boot, which hasn't budged an inch all these months, through snow and rains and now this extraordinary tempest that sends me running to shut the windows. I like dangerous weather like this, days so dark and violent the world seems ready to blow apart or be transformed into something else; thick, moody, inward days that churn up the buried ghosts inside, and conjure shadowed soulful feelings, *inich* feelings, the Germans call them, like Schwartzkopf's bittersweet descrescendo singing the last of the "Four Last Songs."

Shortly after ten o'clock, Sullivan calls to say that his California lead is "very much alive," but jerking him around. He's been strangely secretive about his suspect and refuses to answer detailed questions, telling me that there are some things I'm better off not knowing. I don't know what Sullivan means by this but am learning to let him be the boss, preserve the cloak-and-dagger routine that his ego seems to require. Also, I've had no response to the letter I sent off to Washington. Either my photo and letter are lying in some bureaucratic slush pile with thousands of other pleas from abandoned children or not even Big Brother can track down my father. The next possibility is too sad to consider: that the letter arrived in my father's hands and he chose not to contact me. I'd rather he turned out to be dead.

After Louis showers and goes to work, I take Marcia's shoebox from the top of the closet where I keep it hidden, clear my desk, remove the box top, and look inside at the few things I found in her drawer the week she died. This is the day I remember her, the day I bring her back to the world. Every year, on the anniversary of her death, I set Marcia's things out and look at them in candle-light. She seems especially present to me lately. Perhaps it's be-cause I'm remembering so much, looking back, imagining Jim. In moments of tenderness, dread, nostalgia, watching Louis's face as he sleeps with bad dreams, sitting too long in Doctor G's office when fear overtakes me, Marcia seems closer than ever before. Still it's hard for me to believe, even after all these years, that my good-hearted sister is gone for good, and that this handful of random objects is all that remains of her in this world outside the confines of memory.

There's a half-finished journal, the sort you'd buy in a Hall-mark card shop, with a tiny, broken gold lock; a yellow legal pad bent in half, filled with recipes for simple dishes (beef stew, fet-tucine Alfredo), and crossed-out lists of things to do (fix brakes, buy shampoo) written in Marcia's careful hand; and three old photographs. In the first image, Marcia, Joyce, and I are on the lawn of a municipal park, feeding pigeons, my hair buzzed into the "butch" Mom forced me to get for kindergarten. In the second photo, a Polaroid, Marcia is standing in our front yard wearing pointed white high heels and a graduation gown, hair flipped under a mortarboard. In the last photo, my favorite, Marcia wears the blue velvet dress we helped her pick out for the prom. I sat on the floor with Joyce, Belle, and Mom while the seamstress pinned the hem of the gown, Marcia spinning model-like in front of a three-way mirror. That dress had been a gift from Milty, who lived in Akron with his new family, and in the photo the blue velvet shines over Marcia's ample bust, a corsage pinned to her elbow-high glove. Her date stands next to her in his tuxedo, a pale-faced, red-haired boy, holding her arm as the two of them smile at the Coconut Grove, next to a set of fake palm trees. Marcia never looked lovelier than on the night that picture was taken, as if her life had peaked for an hour, captured now in a single snapshot. I lean the picture against the wall and light a *yahrzeit* candle close by. The image turns gold in the dark room. The tree branches scratch at my window like claws.

I was the person she came to for help. At the time, I could not understand why Marcia chose me of all people to approach in her final distress. Later I began to suspect that I was the only man she trusted.

She came to see me the last time in the middle of a January afternoon, when she was twenty-nine and I was twenty, home at Bob's house for a college break. I was reading at the kitchen table when a knock at the window startled me. Marcia had cut her hair short in the two months since I'd seen her, and her wrinkled clothes were covered with cat hair. Her face was creased, her eyes bloodshot. When I opened the door, she stayed in the threshold, and when I put my arms around her, she leaned against me without hugging back.

"What's wrong?" I asked, but Marcia just shook her head.

"Tell me what's the matter," I said, meaning *immediately* the matter. She'd been shakier than usual that year, after Milty's sudden death—which affected her deeply though Marcia hardly knew him—and then her husband's great betrayal. This hadn't been mere philandering; what happened to Marcia was sociopathic, a domestic act of such cruelty that we barely believed her story at first. Marcia had been married before, at eighteen, to a classmate from her community college who had a penchant for using his fists. When his temper tantrums left her bruised, she made excuses for his behavior, but after five years she'd given up. When a customer at the bank where she worked—a chubby bald man with a funny mustache—gave her his number in case she ever needed a friend, he seemed so kind that Marcia called Steve and met him sometimes for lunch in the park. She told him the truth about her life—she wasn't afraid to talk to a stranger, just as Mom once confided to Julie—and after a few months of these secret meetings, Steve persuaded Marcia to leave her husband and live with him.

We were all happy to see this happen; Steve seemed like a miracle man whom chance had sent to rescue Marcia. After she was divorced and married Steve, he endeared himself to the family and seemed to dote on his wounded bride. For two years they appeared to be happy, till one day Steve announced that he was ill. His doctor had found liver cancer, he said; the tumor was advanced and aggressive, and treatment would require him to spend three nights a week at a hospital. Marcia was devastated by this and wanted to sleep at the hospital with him, but Steve wouldn't hear of it. He wanted to protect her, he said, so Marcia let him go by himself.

Nine months passed while Marcia worried desperately. Her husband was gone three nights a week, but strangely he never seemed to get worse. When my mother remarked on how healthy he looked, Steve told her that the treatments were working. We were relieved for him, of course, but even more relieved for Marcia. She'd been prone to depression since childhood. Like somebody without skin, Marcia absorbed all the pain around her and could hardly read a newspaper without having to go to bed afterward. In a house full of big personalities, she'd been the dogged, obedient daughter, forced as the oldest child to shoulder the burdens that Mom was ill-equipped to handle. Long before her first marriage, she'd taken a great deal of abuse, and we'd feared what effect her new husband's death might have on her fragile psyche. The crisis, however, seemed to be passing.

It's hard to fathom what happened next. Marcia found the note after work, informing her that there'd been no cancer—no illness at all—just a woman Steve loved more than he loved her, and with whom he'd been sleeping all these months when he was supposed to be hospitalized. He wanted to marry this woman posthaste if Marcia would sign the attached papers and send them to a p.o. box in Carmel.

She snapped. A lifetime of emotional pounding and breaches

of trust reached an unbearable pitch. With Aunt Ruth's help, Marcia found a psychiatrist who put her into a locked ward and kept her there for several weeks with no visitors allowed. When Marcia seemed a bit stronger, she was moved to a place with lawns and trees where we visited her on Sunday mornings. I remember thinking how peaceful she seemed in those protected surroundings; or perhaps it was thanks to her therapist, a large black woman named Amy, who sat with us on a bench in the shade talking about taking tiny steps—just *this much* every day, she said, fingers an inch apart as Marcia nodded in agreement. Leaving after one hospital visit, I sincerely believed that Marcia was mending, so that when she called me in a panic at school two weeks later to say that they were discharging her on the orders of her insurance company—and that she wasn't ready—I was furious. I begged my mother to challenge the claim—as a minor, I was helpless—but there was little she could do. In fact, she believed that this tack might be better, that Marcia was stronger than she thought—*her mother's daughter*, is how Mom put it—and that learning to cope without being coddled, just as Ida had, would do Marcia good.

At twenty, drunk on youthful pride and Bob's credo of success, I convinced myself that she'd find her way, that somehow Marcia's spirit would right itself. I truly believed that the will to live would prevail if a person just persevered and put one foot in front of the other. I believed that however impossible life might seem, we were meant to endure it regardless, to go on although we couldn't go on, as Samuel Beckett would say, drawing strength from sheer instinct. I couldn't survive without that belief, I was too close to the edge myself, and convinced myself that Marcia would come to the same conclusion sooner or later in spite of how afraid she was.

Now she was leaning against the oven in Bob's kitchen, wrapped in a bulky Mexican sweater, looking confused and ill. I offered her the chair next to mine.

"What's the matter?" I asked her again. "Talk to me."

Marcia sat down. At first she said nothing. Her bottom lip was chapped and trembling. Then she asked in a voice like a child's, "How do you do it, Mark?"

"Do what?"

Marcia looked at me and said, "Live."

I didn't know what to answer her. "You just do."

She shook her head.

"You have to," I said.

"I can't."

"Yes, you can." I pushed the hair from Marcia's eyes to make her feel better. Her bangs were lank with dandruff and sweat. I pulled a comb from my back pocket and ran it through her hair, the way she'd let me do as a boy.

"Remember 'Tar Baby'?" Marcia asked. She used to read to me from O. Henry, Aesop, Edgar Allan Poe. The story of Tar Baby was one of my favorites.

"And Little Black Sambo."

Then in a barely audible voice, Marcia told me, "I want to die."

"Don't say that."

"I do." She said this with no drama at all; her tone was flat and calm and clear.

"Everyone does a little. Sometimes."

"Not like that."

"Like how, Marcia?"

Slowly, she began to tell me what it was like to be in her head. She said that indifference cut her like knife blades, the everyday coldness and cruelty of people trapped in their locked-away cells without touching or caring for those around them. She said everyday sadness was crushing her, that she couldn't breathe and didn't belong here. As she talked, waves of blackness poured over me, the blackness I remembered from childhood, oozing it seemed through the walls of the house, a down-sucking force of waste and grief and women at the ends of their ropes. I'd fought with every muscle I had not to be buried by this dark tide, but its remnants were still inside me. I felt the seductive tug as she spoke, the self-destructive urge to go limp, give up and sink down—a welcome sensation like drowning. But even as this depression beckoned, I kicked and struggled to the surface. I stood and walked away from her. At a safe distance, the suction released so that I could catch my breath.

"Tell me what happened," I said.

"I went up on the roof today."

"What roof?"

"At the bank. Today at lunch, to see how it felt. I sat on the edge with my legs hanging over."

I stared at her.

"It was so far down," Marcia told me, "I could hardly see the sidewalk. I saw a baby in a stroller. I thought I saw Mom. Don't tell anyone."

I didn't know what to say to her; the image of my sister thirty floors up with her legs over the side of the roof shocked me too much to let me utter a word. I did not phone an ambulance; I did not phone her therapist, or Mom, or Aunt Ruth, or anyone who might have helped her. Instead of putting her somewhere safe, acting in some way appropriate to the dire warning she'd come to give me, I kept my mouth shut and convinced myself that Marcia would never do it, not really. I reminded myself of what I'd been told, that people who threaten to kill themselves don't; later that day, Bob repeated this line and compared her to the boy who cried wolf. Surely she'd bottomed out this time, I thought; surely she'd rally back to the living. This is what I told myself as I walked Marcia to her car that evening, not knowing that this was a fatal mistake. But could I have stopped what happened next had I kept her away from that empty apartment? Who but God could answer that question?

Five days later, the telephone rang: Belle was shrieking. She'd found Marcia face down in the bedroom of her apartment, hand reaching out toward the telephone. The shades were drawn, five empty pill bottles strewn on the floor. Her cat was crying under the bed. There was no note.

I ran across the parking lot of the hospital where I was born and found Mom and Belle on a bench outside the ER. Mom looked frozen; Belle was sobbing.

"They won't tell us," Belle said.

I went to the desk and demanded to be told what was happening. The nurse refused to give me the details.

"Where is she?"

"Who are you?"

I walked through the swinging doors as the nurse called after me, past patients on stretchers in the hallway, past empty beds and cubicles full of people, into a large room partitioned with blue curtains. A guard came after me, ordering me to leave, but I kept going, looking for her. The guard grabbed my shoulder just as I reached the far end of the room. Marcia was naked to the waist, breasts exposed, eyes open but fixed. Her body was raised, one side of her mouth clamped open with thick tubing running down her throat. There were tubes in both nostrils, an IV in her arm, and strangely shaped black adhesive patches stuck to various parts of her chest. Her breasts rose and fell but she wasn't breathing. Machines blipped, electric lines crested and flattened on the screen. Her hands were folded in her lap; the gold band was back on her wedding finger. When I said her name, there was no response. Not a flicker.

"She can't hear you," a doctor said.

I put my mouth next to Marcia's ear and said her name.

"She's gone," said the doctor.

I sat on the floor. I touched Marcia's foot—it was soft and warm—then heard the whisk of the curtain behind me as the doctor pulled it closed. The floor felt glacial through my jeans. I wanted it to freeze me through.

Joyce came as soon as she could. We waited at the hospital for seventy-two hours, dozing in chairs, pacing the halls outside the ICU. The second day, a woman appeared with a form requesting Marcia's vital organs. Mom asked me what she should do; I gave her a pen and told her to sign. Aunt Ruth and Grandpa came and went, but the four of us were alone with this, drawn close together like cows in a storm, heads in a tight, locked circle. We'd never felt this close before.

"Code blue, ICU!" Each time we heard this announced over the loudspeaker, I raced to Marcia's glassed-in room, where—if the code had been called on her—a team would be surrounding her bed, shouting, applying electric paddles that made Marcia's body lurch up from the mattress. Then they'd pound on her chest till they got a heartbeat. I begged them to leave her alone, but the law required extraordinary measures for the three days until brain death could be declared. When the code was over, we'd cover her up, fix Marcia's tubes. Mom would wipe the sweat off her forehead with shaking hands. She called her *my baby*—I choked when she said it. If only she'd said this to Marcia before—but I stopped this thought fast, before the explosion of blame could consume me.

When the respirator was finally unplugged, a twilight zone descended upon us, disabling everybody but me. While the rest of the family stared at the walls, I booked the cremation, haggled with lawyers. This was the first time I'd realized that crisis acted paradoxically on me; in the midst of hysteria, I grew almost unnaturally calm. I solved problems and took care of business while everyone else fell apart. In Aunt Ruth's living room on the day of the memorial service, I gave Marcia's eulogy before a handful of family and friends, talked about her gentleness, her humor and enormous compassion. I warned against thinking that Marcia had failed—and against feeling bitter toward her choice, however much we might miss her—then recited a poem that Belle found folded up in Marcia's wallet:

> *Do not stand at my grave and weep.*
> *I am not there. I do not sleep.*
> *I am a thousand winds that blow.*
> *I am the diamond glints on snow.*
> *I am the sunlight on ripened grain.*
> *I am the gentle autumn rain.*
> *When you awaken in the morning's hush,*
> *I am the swift uplifting rush*
> *Of quiet birds in circled flight,*
> *I am the stars that shine at night.*
> *Do not stand at my grave and cry,*
> *I am not there, I did not die.*

As I spoke, Belle supported my back with her hand, Mom leaned on Grandpa's shoulder and sobbed—the first time I'd seen them touch this way—and Joyce held Emma's arm. Uncle Marty sat in his wheelchair, hands jerking, tears running down a face twisted by Parkinson's; my cousin Ronnie stood behind him, holding Uncle Marty's shoulders. After I finished speaking, I hugged whoever needed it and helped the women serve bagels and lox.

I didn't grieve—I couldn't grieve. I told myself brave stories instead, about how Marcia had seized her fate, taken life into her own hands, ceased being a victim and turned into a martyr instead. I told myself that she was a hero for daring to step into the unknown, and imagined her death as a victory. It seemed selfish to want her back for our sake when we'd done so little to help her when she was alive. Numbed by this armor of heroic fiction, I didn't let my sadness show and took practical action instead. With Belle's help, I set about emptying Marcia's apartment. We folded her clothes into garbage bags, stacked her dishes in cardboard boxes, gave her cat to an elderly neighbor. At the back of a drawer by Marcia's bedside, hidden under some magazines, I found the locked journal before me now, with a doll-sized key attached to a string. When Belle left, I inserted the key. The pages were neatly dated and headed with large-lettered do's and don'ts like chapters in a self-help book. *DON'T BE SO ANGRY* one page declared; *REMEMBER IT'S NOT THEIR FAULT* read another. I wondered who *they* were, and then found a brief passage in which I was mentioned, on a page headed *LEARN TO BE HAPPY*: *"Mark called today. He seems so happy. I want to be happy too but there's something wrong (rotten) with me. Amy says this is stinkin' thinkin'. Sometimes I hate Amy. When I told her that she said it was good. She says she wants me to hate her more. I don't know why, she's my only friend. Why don't I understand anything?"*

The passages I skimmed were filled with loneliness and recrimination—their naked pain almost too wounding to bear. Then on the page dated 9/28/76, Marcia's twenty-eighth birthday, the handwriting suddenly changed from fluid and neat to square and erratic. Under a heading marked *GET MAD*, she wrote: *"Amy says it's good to get mad. She says when I don't get mad I get sad and if I want to get better, I have to let it all out. Okay, I HATE THEIR FUCKING GUTS! THEY'RE MEAN AND SELF-ISH AND I WANT TO KILL THEM!"* Again I wondered who *them* could be, but instead of explaining, Marcia felt guilty. *"How can I say that?"* she wrote on the next page. *"I love them and they love me—underneath. But they made me like this before I could stop them. Mom—and Jim most of all."*

Jim? My father? I reread the passage and couldn't imagine what other Jim she could have meant. What could my father have done to "make" Marcia the way she was? A few pages later, under *NO MORE SHAME,* I found this: *"I talked to Amy about Jim and the shame. Why do I still think of that?? I know it's wrong, Mom should have stopped him. We shouldn't have gone . . ."* But just there, after the verb, the writing ended and the following pages were torn out. I counted the edges—six missing pages. The rest of the journal held nothing but sketchy notations, no more bold headings or affirmations, no mention of family, just halfhearted musings trailing off, on 1/14/77, with the four words: *"Nobody knows but me."*

Today, with Marcia's candlelit picture propped up in front of me, I open the journal again to those pages where Jim's name is mentioned and ask myself what could have happened to make Marcia write those things. How could my father have caused her such shame? Could there have been some kind of abuse? I have few clues to help me decide, and yet, seen with a detective's eye, the troubles signs are hard to ignore. A twelve-year-old girl, unloved by her father, ignored by her mother, worshipping this tall handsome man; a man without mooring, alone (as they must have been alone sometimes) with a girl who isn't really his daughter, pretty, in bangs and bobby socks, submissive in a way his wife was not, a girl in whose melancholic eyes he saw his beaten-down, out-of-work self reflected back large and powerful. I'm troubled by what part husbandly revenge might have played in this scene, the grudge my father held against a woman who couldn't love him, and what lengths this revenge might have led him to on a lonely day when the house was empty and the two of them were out of sight, wounded people needing affection, and turned against the same distant woman.

I wonder now, should my father appear, if I will confront him with these questions, perhaps even show him this journal. You might ask yourself why any man would confess to violating a twelve-year-old girl, three decades after the fact, but I've seen the reason with my own eyes. Three years ago in a New Jersey suburb, researching an exposé about incest, I sat in a kindergarten classroom with five convicted male child-molesters, out on bail or about to serve time, and listened to them talk in a circle with their therapist about the girls they had raped—five respectable-seeming men who, in times of stress, anger, drinking, or marital crisis, had crossed the line of decency with daughters and stepdaughters they claimed to adore—their "favorites"—blighting, without meaning to, both the girls' lives and their own. I wanted to hate these men but I couldn't, sitting there in a classroom surrounded eerily by miniature chairs and walls covered with crayon drawings. I understood, without wanting to, how easily boundaries could be erased in the course of everyday human weakness, how good people did godawful things which they paid for the rest of their lives. I listened as one by one they confessed, not only the full extent of their crimes but the gratitude and relief they felt at being able to publicly voice secrets they had held inside like vials of poison.

I remember thinking how much one of these guys, a grease monkey in gas station coveralls, with black hair slicked off his handsome face, and blue eyes the color of his uniform, reminded me of what my father might have looked like, down to the crud underneath his thumbnails. I listened to him describe how he'd fallen, caught in a frigid marriage, doted on by his only daughter—*daddy's little girl*, he called her—a twelve-year-old who sat on his lap and began to massage his neck one night when he'd had too much to drink, then allowed him to touch her between the legs. "I never wanted to hurt her," he said of the years of sex that followed between them, and although his behavior repulsed me, I knew that he was telling the truth. After my interviews were over, he gave me a lift to the train station and told me that his daughter had finally agreed to write to him after five years of unbearable silence. When we shook hands on the station platform, this stranger said to me, "I never thought I'd be standing here," meaning, I knew, in such dire straits. "But here I am."

I wrote those words down afterward alongside a quote I've always loved, describing how each of us comes to wisdom. "Every journey has a secret destination of which the traveler is unaware." Thinking of Martin Buber's words now, I wonder what destination I'm bound for, in search of someone who may have hurt Marcia. I touch the edges of the journal's torn-out pages, look at Marcia's teenage face, smudged where the photograph has wrinkled, and cry for her till my jaw aches and my guts feel as if they've been trampled. It hurts to remember her tenderness, the pain she lived with all those years. It hurts to remember how good Marcia was and how she tried to protect me and Belle. The pain makes Marcia seem very close, as if I'm moving toward her now, crossing a river of lies and secrets with half an oar and a sinking boat, over to the place where she's waiting. When I close my eyes, I can see her there, the way I saw her once in a dream. There had been a knock on the door of the bedroom—I rose to open it. Marcia was standing on the threshold, smiling and radiant, next to a tall man. She put her arms around my neck, pulled me close, and whispered *I'm fine*. It was Marcia's voice, her body, her breath, vivid and unmistakable, real as an actual visitation. I opened my eyes electrified, extremely happy, as if she'd come to relieve me of guilt and tell me that she had landed safely. Or perhaps she was preparing me somehow for the stormy day of my own crossing. I look out the window now at the rainclouds; the chimes are ringing like an alarm, the tree whipping against the roof, but still the black boot has not moved. The candle burns steadily down in its glass. Visitation or simply a dream, I wonder now if I'm being guided by Marcia's outstretched, invisible hand.

· thirty-four ·

"Joyce is hysterical!" Belle says on the phone. It's the middle of the night, a few weeks after Marcia's anniversary. Louis is next to me on the futon, clutching a pillow around his head after being jolted from a sound sleep. Voices from Marie's TV set are vibrating through the floor. The digital clock says 2:31.

"What's wrong?"

"Oh my God, you won't believe this." Belle then tells me that the girl Joyce gave up for adoption twenty-two years ago has contacted her out of the blue. Joyce has just called Belle, delirious; the girl wants to meet her right away. I'm too groggy from sleeping pills, too stunned by the fact of this happening now, to know how to respond at first.

"What's she going to *think*?" Belle asks.

"Jesus Christ," I say. What Belle means is this: how is a girl who's searched for her mother, probably at some expense, going to react to the news that Joyce is in a homeless shelter in North Carolina, waiting for the staples in her head to be removed after her toothless trucker boyfriend bashed in her head with a monkey wrench?

"It gets worse."

"It can't," I say.

"The girl is an orthodox Jew."

"You're lying."

"She cried on the phone to Joyce. She said that finding her was the happiest day of her life."

"Somebody's got to warn her," I say.

"If this girl rejects her, Joyce will lose it."

"Too late for that."

"Like Marcia."

"Don't say that."

"I'm scared," Belle answers.

I remember when Joyce went away. I was six, Joyce was fourteen, and suddenly one day she was gone. Mom told us that she'd gone to camp but I didn't ask too many questions. I was glad that Joyce wasn't there. Without her ordering us around, griping at Mom, bullying Marcia, the little apartment seemed twice the size. I knew that I was supposed to love Joyce, even though she was so mean to me, and pity her because she was fat, but I was happy she'd disappeared.

Time passed—I don't know how long—then one day with no warning whatever, Mom said that Joyce was coming home. The four of us piled into the T-Bird and drove downtown on the Hollywood freeway, then cruised up and down wide streets with big lawns in search of the address. Marcia read the directions; Belle stood up and leaned out the convertible, stick-thin legs and a sundress up to her *pupik*. I hoped we wouldn't find the house.

"There she is!" Belle squealed. Joyce was waiting on the front step of an enormous porch, hunched with her knees up under her chin. She'd cut her hair and pushed it behind her ears and was wearing a dress I'd never seen. Mom honked the horn and Joyce stood up, then lumbered across the lawn with her suitcase. She got in the car without saying a word—just got in the back, stuck Belle on her lap, and looked out in the other direction.

Finally Marcia said, "Hi, Joycie."

"Hi," said Joyce.

None of us talked the whole way home.

After Mom had left the room, Joyce told us about the baby. She'd named her Tina Marie—the father was probably one of the guys I saw kissing her at the roller rink when their friends weren't looking—and as Joyce described how pretty her little girl was, weeping as she spoke, I felt close to her for perhaps the first time. "They let me hold her for an hour. She was so tiny."

"Why did they take her?" I asked.

"Mommy made them."

There was something about this that I couldn't grasp, the finality of taking a child, and Joyce never seeing her baby again. In my six-year-old mind, it didn't make sense that a part of you could wander off—or be carried away somewhere—forever. How could a person just disappear? When Joyce told us the story about saying good-bye to her baby, my mind stopped at the forever point, thinking the girl would come back someday, that somehow they'd see each other again. Just as in a secret part of myself, I believed that I might see my father.

The meeting is planned for a Sunday morning, since Joyce's daughter can't travel on the Sabbath. Mom sends Joyce the bus fare for the trip across-country from North Carolina. Meanwhile, Devorah—that's her daughter's name—will fly in from Chicago with her husband and children. Belle gives me a detailed report.

"I'm a grandma!" Joyce says while they wait for Devorah at Grandpa's house, the only kosher home in the family. Mom has bought Joyce respectable clothes, but Joyce is clearly terrified. "What if she doesn't like me?" Joyce asks.

"She'll like you, you're her mother," says Emma, as if these things followed like night and day.

"I lost her once already," Joyce says.

"You can't lose the same thing twice," says Emma.

The first thing Devorah says when she walks through the door and sees Joyce is, "Now I know where I come from!" She's heavy-set and loud like Joyce, with curly hair and small eyes. When she throws her arms around Joyce's shoulders, both of them howl with the same shoulder-shaking motion, and when they raise their hands to comfort each other, the same pouch of flesh hangs from the tricep, covered with small red dots.

"You must be Great Grandpa!" she says, turning to the only *yarmulke* in the room.

"Hello, dahling."

"Come on in, kids! Meet your great-great grandpa! And this is my husband, Morrie!" A thin man with a scraggly black beard and glasses shakes Grandpa's hand, then pecks at Joyce's cheek between rivulets of her dripping mascara. Two sleepy-looking girls cling to his legs, wearing matching white shoes and headbands.

"I'm Ida," Mom says in her husky voice. Joyce's daughter shouts "Grandma!" and hugs her tight. My mother looks mortified.

When the introductions are over, Emma and Aunt Ruth serve tea and cake in the formal dining room while they all stare awkwardly at one another. It's obvious that Devorah's initial enthusiasm is beginning to settle. She's studying Joyce up and down out of the corner of her eye, from the blue patent leather Kinney pumps to the black-and-blue marks on Joyce's neck, creeping through the pancake makeup. When Joyce tries to lure her newfound grandchildren into her lap, the girls cling more tightly to Morrie's pant legs, and Devorah doesn't encourage them to come forward. Joyce is mopping at her brow with a napkin, completely unsure of how to behave. The more nervous she gets, the louder and more aggressive she is, till she seems to have forgotten completely where she is and who is present. To everyone's horror, desperate to say *something*, Joyce launches into a travelogue of her life on the road with toothless Phil, crashed out in sleeping bags on the back of his flatbed, showering in truck-stop bathrooms. Joyce has moved in that milieu for so many years that she has no idea how distasteful her life sounds, and when the others try to change the subject, she dominates the floor and won't shut up.

"Have you ever been in a truck stop, honey?" she asks Devorah, who's wearing a black velvet hat and a lace-collared blouse.

Devorah shakes her head, speechless. "You're lucky! Jee-zus! I wish I hadn't either," Joyce says, trying to sound cheerful.

Devorah looks furtively at her husband.

"Life's what you make it," says Aunt Ruth. "Don't you think so, dear?"

Devorah nods.

"Life sucks and then you die," says Joyce.

Morrie shakes his head, pulls the girls closer to him.

"I have that on a T-shirt," Joyce says, desperately trying to turn it into a joke.

Nobody laughs—it's too late to laugh. In less than an hour, the whole thing is over. Devorah takes Morrie's hand and together they herd the girls to the opposite side of the room where Grandpa is, and try to persuade him to talk about his boyhood in Russia, which he's done his best to forget. When Devorah asks Grandpa if he ever feels nostalgia for his roots, he looks at her like she's insane. Aunt Ruth, who could charm a cuddle from the Marquis de Sade, places herself between Devorah and Morrie to show them a family photo album, pointing out those who are missing, Ronnie, Shelley, Marcia, Marty, and Grandma Bella, while Joyce, Mom, and Belle watch them from afar. After they've finished looking at pictures, and picking at Emma's cheese and crackers, Devorah looks at her watch and makes an excuse to leave.

"So soon?" Joyce asks.

"The girls . . ." says Devorah. She holds out her hand for Joyce to shake. When Joyce tries to hug her, Devorah keeps her hands at her sides.

"I hoped we could talk some," Joyce says.

"Maybe next time," the young woman answers.

"I named you Tina Marie," Joyce blurts out.

"Oh," says Devorah. "That's pretty."

"I never would have . . ." Joyce says then, but stops herself. Devorah is looking over her shoulder toward the door, a nervous smile stuck on her face as everyone watches what's happening. "Never mind," Joyce says.

"It's good to meet you," says Devorah.

"Let's stay in touch," says Joyce. "Okay?"

"Okay," she answers. But anyone can see that Devorah doesn't mean it. When she walks out the door she'll be gone for good, only this time the tables will be turned: it will be her choice not to know her mother, the daughter's choice to close the door. She'll fly back to Chicago and be grateful that the religious people who adopted her are her real parents. She may even regret ever starting her search, having seen the person Joyce is, and begin to be bothered by things in herself that she might have overlooked before— but having met her reflection in Joyce, no longer can. How will I feel if my father turns out to be someone I find repulsive, I wonder, a broken-down drunk in a trailer park, say, or a con man, or a spineless prick? How glad will I be to have found him *then?* Will knowing who he really is cause me shame, as I imagine Devorah feels in front of her husband? Or am I in for a better surprise?

As for Joyce, when she thinks of this day later on, waiting for phone calls that never come, long after Devorah has her number disconnected, Joyce will say that she doesn't blame her. She'll ask *who'd want me for a mother?* and lay this second loss of her child on the mass of failures she drags behind her, the baby she handed to strangers that day, the other baby found dead in his crib, the children she's given birth to since then in marriages lasting a year or two, children who hardly speak to her now, whose lives have mirrored Joyce's own, from homeless shelters to twelve-step meetings, and falling back off the wagon again. After Devorah walks out, Joyce looks through Emma's embroidered curtains at the grandchildren she'll never know, who didn't so much as sit on her lap or kiss her cheek before they skipped out. Belle puts her arms round Joyce's shoulders. Mom stands next to them, hands at her sides, looking small and helpless and lost.

· thirty-five ·

My best friend Robert calls from Santa Fe for a progress report on Mac Sullivan. Robert and I are best friends now that we're no longer lovers, closer to brothers than anything else, though he's moved two thousand miles away. I tell him how annoyed I am that the detective is making such slow progress; Robert reminds me, *as he would*, that patience has never been my virtue. I remind him that it's not *his* father being tracked like Sasquatch through the streets of Pasadena. Robert's father, Lou, is a saint, the kind of old-world, street-smart Jew who carries a thousand bucks cash in a fanny pack just so he can cash his kids' checks. He is the father that I would have chosen, of all the fathers that I've ever met— twelve years after I broke up with Robert, Lou still kisses me when we meet and tells me I'm his adopted son. I've always wished that it was legally binding.

"How's David?" Robert asks.

David is Joyce's son, who didn't come to meet his half-sister. Robert does not understand my family; he says we remind him of Jewish Okies. "No show," I say.

"What about the other one?" he asks, meaning Kyla Juanita May Clay, Joyce's daughter from a short-lived marriage to a black man. Kyla, unmarried, recently had twin boys at fifteen.

"Disappeared into the ether," I say.

"Oy," says Robert. Across two time zones, I hear him thinking how happy he is not to be in my clan.

"Nothing changes," I say.

"David was such a wonderful boy," Robert says before we hang up.

Thirteen years ago, David had come to stay with us in the Hell's Kitchen loft I shared with Robert. He was tall for the sixth grade, with a smushed-in nose, coppery hair, and sweet brown eyes that looked like Marcia's. I'd moved to New York the previous year, and David had begged to visit. Since his own father lived fifty miles away and came to see him very rarely, David was especially attached to me, his *cool uncle*, who gave him books, clothes, and a see-through skateboard, and soaked with him in Bob's hot tub. He reminded me of myself at his age, curious, awkward, funny, smart, with all the cards stacked against him. Joyce was even more unstable than Mom had been, moving David and Kyla from town to town with her no-good-man-of-the-moment, and I worried that her son would lose his way, if he even managed to find it. He needed someone to show him that there was a world outside the caved-in one that Joyce lived in, where intelligent people led interesting lives, and good things were possible for a boy who went after what he wanted. He was eager to learn and full of questions, and after I moved to New York, he wrote me long, large-printed letters about how bad things were at home and how he needed to come and see me.

I sent David a round-trip ticket, and within hours of arriving he'd settled into our loft as if he belonged there. While the three of us were watching TV one night, he rolled over sleepy-eyed in his briefs and asked if he could come live with us. "Please, Uncle Mark, I hate it there," he said meaning the place where Joyce was squatting. "I want to come and live with you."

I looked at Robert for some clue of what to say. Could I possibly take care of David, be a replacement father to him? Robert seemed to like the idea; he'd always wanted a child and had even thought of fathering one with a woman friend from his college days who fell for unpaternal men. But I knew in my heart that I couldn't do it. I'd never seriously thought of being a father; the prospect of that dependency, twenty-four hours a day, was something I doubted I could withstand. It was all I could do to half-please a lover—Robert felt gypped as it was, with me working my eighteen-hour days and giving the bulk of my passion to writing. Yet here was Robert nodding at me, wanting me to say yes. I told David that this was a big decision and I'd have to give it some serious thought.

What actually preoccupied me was how to tell this wonderful boy that I didn't want him. During the next week, Robert realized that I was beyond convincing, and though he was willing to help with David, he couldn't take him on by himself. Besides, it was me that David wanted; somehow I needed to send him home without feeling that I was abandoning him. But each time I might have made the speech—crossing the river to Ellis Island, on the roof of the World Trade Center, alone with him in a boat on the lake in Central Park, taking turns rowing across the lake, I couldn't bring myself to do it. David didn't ask again; maybe he knew the answer already but hoped that I would change my mind.

One night while he was asleep on the sofa, a box of cookies next to his hand and my childhood copy of *The Adventures and Discoveries of Marco Polo* propped open in his lap, I asked myself what was wrong with me, why I couldn't reach out to this boy, my own nephew, when he needed help? How had I become a man who could paddle away from someone drowning rather than making room in the lifeboat and take a chance on sinking together? But at twenty-six, obsessed by ambition, desperate to make a name for myself, to prove that I was *somebody*, I was too caught up in my own survival to act any differently. My future was all-important to me; success mattered more than anything, including the welfare of my nephew, however much I claimed to love him. Perhaps I was my father's son after all, able to do what he'd done to me—though David wasn't technically mine—and go on living, as I assumed Jim had. With David sleeping peacefully, I experienced one of those fluorescent moments of standing naked before your own conscience, excuses and fantasies stripped away, faced with the bare facts of who you are. When David woke up the next morning, I told him, gently as I could, that there was no way he could live with me. He didn't try to persuade me at all— he got quiet for half an hour, then told me on the way to the airport that the next time Joyce's boyfriend beat up on him, he'd just have to run away on his own. I promised I'd have a talk with Joyce and that I'd send him a ticket that summer to come back and visit for a month, but David didn't seem to believe me. He hugged me quickly at the gate, shouldered his knapsack, and ran through the door to the jetway. That summer, I broke up with Robert and had no money for David's plane fare; in fact, it would be seven years before we saw each other again, in the Montana boonies where David was living.

Now I wonder what might have happened if I'd made a different decision that day, opened my door and let him in. I ask myself whether fathering David might not have made me a better man, taught me lessons a dozen years ago which I've barely begun to learn today. Would fathering David have given us both roots, taught me commitment, made me less selfish, grown me into a more stable person? And what sort of life might David have had if I'd given him shelter when he needed it instead of leaving him to his fate?

These thoughts leave me sad and confused. I wonder if David would be interested if I were to offer him a home now. On impulse I call the last number he gave me, somewhere in Oklahoma. A computer tells me that the line's been disconnected.

· thirty-six ·

At the beginning of June, six months after the search for my father began, Louis and I make a snap decision to spend the summer in Santa Fe. He's ready to leave the flower business: after twelve years of thorn-slashed fingers and rich ladies *hocking* him over his tulips, he's had enough. He wants to be unemployed for a while, blow his savings, take a risk, have some fun after this stressful year. I need a break from New York too, from Sullivan and plagues and impotent doctors. A run-in I had with Doctor G convinced me that I was in the wrong place. After Barbara showed me an item in *Time* magazine about an experimental drug being tested in Sweden with unprecedented results—and trials being done in the States—I showed the piece to Doctor G and asked him to sign me up. He patted my hand and told me not to believe what I read in the papers. His tone was so condescending, his response to good news so uninspiring, that I realized, once and for all, that visiting him was bad for my health, especially since his treatments were useless. I preferred to take my chances without him and regain some normalcy in my life.

We place an ad in a downtown paper and screen thirty applicants for the apartment, finally choosing a sweet, sparrow-faced woman in her thirties named Sandy, here on assignment with the BBC, who charms us with her lovely voice and instant love of the "quaint atmosphere." She gazes out over the garden, at the man with the cross-shaped scar on his chest sunbathing in boxer shorts on the fire escape, at the doves in the tree, the children playing, and looks in profile like the young Margaret Hamilton with a short haircut and tweed culottes. "Quite adorable," Sandy says, then offers us more money than we're asking, even with the cockroaches, smelly hallway, and one-eyed Marie downstairs pounding the ceiling with her broomstick. We agree to a three-month lease.

On the phone, Sullivan is bouncy as ever, though he's come to a glitch in his reconnaissance: checking Pasadena Jim's bank records, he's discovered that the suspect's files have been purged. Either Pasadena Jim knows that he's being watched, or he's cleared his accounts for some other reason. Sullivan tells me that there's no sense in my waiting around until he gets a positive ID.

We find a cinderblock house perched three miles up an unpaved road, with sweeping views of bone-dry mountains and not a single shade tree in sight. Louis, who spent his teenage summers off from yeshiva competing in the rodeo, takes a three-month lease on an Appaloosa mare he calls Shiksa, and spends his mornings playing cowboy among the arroyos. I sit in the room I've turned into an office and make no progress at all on the book I'm trying to write, about leaving New York, struggling with faith, coming home to bury my friends. I'm too preoccupied with the search to focus. I pour memories into my journal instead, family stories I've nearly forgotten, stories of childhood and adolescence filled with the people whose voices seem close now, those of my sisters and mother, Aunt Ruth and Grandpa, David, and Bruce— even my father, whose face I can finally picture clearly—as if they were circling my desk, humming their stories like a choir. I read books about boys and absent fathers—myths, novels, autobiographies—stare out the window at piñon and sagebrush, and out beyond our stony backyard to the limestone peaks of the Sangre de Cristos, like an overturned dinosaur bordering the desert, kicking its blunt-footed legs toward the sky.

Three weeks after we arrive, while Louis is out at the stable with Shiksa, the telephone rings unexpectedly early. I run for it, thinking it's Barbara or my friend Eve—the only people who call at this hour—but in fact it's a man from the BBC. He tells me that our tenant Sandy—*dear dear Sandra*, he calls her—collapsed and died the previous day on our kitchen floor. In the time it took a friend of hers to run down to the corner to buy a corkscrew, Sandy was stricken and fell. Shocked, I ask the man if he's sure.

"The body was cold when the ambulance came."

"I mean, are you sure that that's how it happened?"

According to her friend's testimony, Sandy had been alone for less than ten minutes, slicing cheese to put on crackers, with the front door locked, in midafternoon. She knew almost no one in New York except this lady in her fifties, who, according to the BBC man, was semi-crippled and a college friend of Sandy's mother in Sissinghurst. Sandra had no enemies, to his knowledge, and seems to have died of a freak infarction. Still, he tells me, to rule out foul play, the NYPD vice squad have sealed off our front door with police tape; no one—including us—is allowed to enter till they've completed their investigation. I tell him how sorry I am for poor Sandy, and hang up the phone feeling shocked, picturing Sandy clutching the sink, her sharp knees buckling, the cheese knife falling, her body crumpling on cheap vinyl tiles with an unassuming thud. I imagine policemen in my kitchen, tramping with black boots and guns and a Polaroid camera, fingering the books on my shelves, looking askance at my gallery of saints, zipping Sandy's too-young corpse into a black plastic morgue bag. I'm reminded again that odds mean nothing—to have picked Sandy out of all those callers!—and that anything at all can happen, statistics and purged files be damned. It startles me to think of my monk's cell as a possible crime scene. Between Mac Sullivan and the NYPD, my life is suddenly crawling with dicks.

· thirty-seven ·

Gisela Turtletaub, our next-door neighbor, comes knocking at the door with an envelope delivered to her by accident.

"They'd need a posse to find their own asshole," Gisela says, meaning the Santa Fe Post Office. Gisela is the Jezebel of Tesuque Road, a bleach-blond, dirty-mouthed Hollywood wife with a huge spread across the way and two young daughters—one perky and platinum, one grim and brunette—whom Louis and I have nicknamed Manic and Depressed.

"Anything important?" Gisela asks, craning her neck to look over my shoulder at the envelope forwarded from New York. "It looks official."

In fact, the envelope in my hand is from a missing person's agency I contacted on a whim shortly before hiring Sullivan. When I realize who the sender is, I tell Gisela—who's always look-

ing for gossip, booze, or *anything* to bring this dusty road to life—
that it's just a work thing, and now I need to get back to my desk.

"You always this antisocial, honey?"

"Quiet these days, that's all."

"Boring!" She pats her mouth, pretending to yawn, then
smiles to let me know she's kidding. "If you ever want to have
some *fun*"—as opposed to what I'm doing, squinting through the
door in a bathrobe—"you know where to find me!"

I open the envelope and find a list of seven living James Matouseks. Three of them have my father's middle initial—an unexpectedly high ratio—with addresses in Utah, Illinois, and Iowa. I
check them against the lists from Sullivan and am surprised to
find that none of them has appeared before. For the first time
since this search began, I question Sullivan's efficiency. Maybe he
isn't covering his bases, maybe he's even wrong about Pasadena
Jim. Also, I'm tired of being so passive, trusting him so unequivo-
cally, sitting here by the phone while he does all the legwork.
Maybe I'm being a patsy, I think, letting him keep me out of the
loop. His assistant Liz has warned me that "the big boss," as she
calls him, is just a control freak, and not to take this personally.
But still, this is *my* father we're looking for. Now, with these new
prospects in hand, I decide to check out these leads for myself
rather than reporting to Sullivan.

I decide to call Iowa Jim first. A creaky old codger answers the
phone. "Hello?"

"Hello," I say. "This is Mark Matousek."

"Matousek? That's my name."

"I know, sir. That's why I'm calling."

"*Why* are you calling?" he asks in a loud voice that lets me know he's hard of hearing.

"Are you James Matousek?" I shout.

"Jim," he says.

"Jim was my father's name," I say.

"That right? Who are you again?"

"I'm calling for a strange reason, Mr. Matousek," I say, feeling increasingly ridiculous.

"Who are you?" he asks again.

"I'm calling you because I'm looking for my father," I say.

He doesn't respond.

"My father's name was Jim, too," I say. "Is there any chance— I mean, are you by any chance my father?"

"Me?"

"I know it's a strange question."

"Hell no, I'm not your father!"

I feel as if I've been slapped, then say— because I have to say something—"Are you absolutely sure?"

He makes a loud spitting noise.

"I don't want anything from you—him—except to talk," I assure him.

"Are you harassing me?"

"No. I'm sorry. I didn't mean to—"

"I've never lived outside this town in my life. You wanna ask my wife? Milly!" he shouts before I can stop him.

"Hello," says an old lady.

I hang up fast, without a word.

Before I can chicken out, I dial the other two James J.'s, who are gentler but equally unhelpful. Both have ironclad alibis, but, unlike Iowa Jim, they're kind and pitying when I tell them who I am and why I'm calling.

"Hey, that's awful sad," says Utah Jim, clucking his tongue like he's passing some road kill. Illinois Jim asks if I have any friends that I can talk to. I'm not prepared for their sympathy and hang up the phone feeling needy and foolish, like an orphan knocking on strangers' doors, looking for handouts and shelter.

A month passes. I write almost nothing. Louis struggles to keep the peace, but my nerves are shot and I'm terrible company. One morning, to get me out of my office, he takes me with him to the stable and does his rodeo routine in the ring, holding his cowboy hat high as he gallops Shiksa around poles and barrels, yodeling like Roy Rogers. Then he saddles up the Appaloosa's sister, a wall-eyed dun named Loca Linda, and leads me into the arroyos—gully-trails snaking through rocky foothills—and out through the mica-flecked dustbowls where we let the horses run. Louis stays a few yards ahead, brushing Shiksa's spotted haunches with the reins, while I, who haven't ridden in years, cling to the saddle horn when he's not looking and try not to be alarmed by the crazed look in Loca Linda's eyes as she jerks her head from side to side and shoots foam from under her bit. Louis slows Shiksa down to a canter and turns her down a sixty-degree embankment toward a copse of poplar trees, waving for me to follow, but Loca refuses to make the descent and runs back toward the barn instead by way of a cactus grove. Louis comes running and heads Loca off as she twirls and starts bucking, slicing my legs on the cactus needles, then finally controls her so that I can throw myself off. I'm laughing too hard to be mad at him, knowing how silly I must have looked, and hobble back to the stable with my hand hooked through his stirrup.

I'm in the bathroom rubbing iodine into my cuts when Mac Sullivan calls to say that Pasadena Jim is definitely my father. There's blood running down my leg onto the linoleum and cotton swabs lining the sink. It stings like hell. I feel almost sick.

"I told you I'm the best," he says, the same way a kid would go na-na-na-na.

"Are you absolutely sure?"

"I bribed the neighbors."

"What did they say?"

"Blue-collar type. Quiet guy. Decent-looking for his age. A loner, more or less—except for the roommate." Sullivan tells me he conned the suspect's unlisted number off of a neighbor and called on a ruse; the other name on the answering machine was a man's. "A *foreigner*," the detective says, as if this is significant.

My leg is stinging unbearably.

"So what happens now?"

"You call the guy!"

Now I truly want to vomit. "I don't know what to say to him."

"Say whatever you want," Sullivan tells me. "Tell him you're his pride and joy. Tell him that he ruined your life." He laughs. "Tell him the truth."

Which one? I want to answer. Instead, I say, "Okay."

"Okay? Is that all the thanks I get?"

"Sorry," I say. "Thanks, Mac."

"You're more than welcome. I'm happy to do it."

"But are you *absolutely* sure?"

"If this isn't your father I'll turn in my license." I hear the incipient edge in his voice—he rankles at having his genius questioned. It's odd to be looking for some way to doubt him, a loophole I can slip through, but rather than feeling glad, I'm weirdly upset and disappointed. It's the kind of disappointment you feel when a wish comes true, the perverse automatic ambivalence prompted by farfetched, answered prayers. For a split second, I'm tempted to tell Mac Sullivan that I've decided to cease and desist. Instead, I take my father's number and promise to call the detective the minute contact has been made.

· thirty-eight ·

I can't bring myself to dial the number. Louis says that I'm over-reacting. He tells me there's nothing to worry about. He says that waiting will make it worse, and that everything will work out fine. I tell him to please snap out of it—he sounds like a goddamn Hallmark card—and that thirty-two years after the fact, I deserve some preparation. I'm not about to punch these digits as if I were calling up for a pizza.

With Louis playing Pasadena Jim, the way they teach you in psychodrama, I run through a list of every *how-will-you-feel-if* that I can think of in response to the inevitable question: Are you my father? I imagine him slamming down the phone, breaking into tears, denying any knowledge of me and Belle, ranting against Mom, launching into a sob story about his life, or lashing out at me on the phone.

"How dare you call me!" I make Louis say.

"What do you mean, how dare I call *you!*" I shout back. "How dare you run away like a coward!"

Louis looks stuck.

"Say something," I say.

"Who're you calling a coward?" he asks.

"Oh, forget it," I say, hanging up my make-believe phone. "What if he's a psycho?" I ask, remembering what Aunt Ruth said about him being "sick in the head."

"Then you'd come by it honestly," Louis says.

"Or what if he's incredibly nice? I should try some happy ones."

I jot down a list of positive responses for Louis to playact, but oddly they're harder to respond to than the nasty ones. I have no idea of what to say to him when he answers my question enthusiastically, or what I might do if my father turns out to be eager to see me right away. What if he's needy or lonely or sick? What if he wants a meaningful relationship or someone to take care of him? What would I say to that?

Louis turns the tables on me. "What do you want, son?"

The word *son* strikes me dumb, as it did when I sat down to write him a letter and found that I had no voice, no vocabulary, with which to address him. "Ga ga," I say.

"Speak English, boy. I'm listening!"

"Let's stop," I say.

"Kiss me, you fool!"

"I mean it!"

"Daddy wants a big smackeroo!" says Louis, coming at me with fish lips.

"Oh, Jesus," I say. "Jesus Christ. What do I say if he asks if I'm married?"

"You tell him the truth."

I hadn't thought of this little glitch. How do I know that my father's not a rabid bigot? What will I do if he damns me to hell, quoting chapter and verse, and tells me he's glad that he never knew me? What do I do if he says something cruel that mimics Mom's old way of comforting me—*you weren't the kind of son that he wanted*. Or what if the opposite proved to be true?

"He could be *married* himself," I say, flipping my hand from side to side.

"No," says Louis.

"He does live with another man. A *foreigner*."

"So?"

"So maybe he's out there playing house with his foreign lover in Pasadena."

"That's nuts."

And yet, this theory could make sense—there are certainly clues to support this conclusion: his flowery signature on the marriage license, his renowned (overcompensating) machismo, his bouts of (guilt-induced) drinking, his chronic lies, inexplicable mood swings, sudden dramatic departure. If my father was indeed gay, and left us to live his authentic life, how could I not forgive him completely, in spite of being abandoned? Playing this out in my mind, our reunion becomes something quite different, a meeting of brothers and possibly friends. I try to picture us on vacation with our boyfriends in Tuscany, marching arm-in-arm with Act Up, visiting Mom at the Happy Valley Farm after they take her away in a van.

"This could be quite a development," I say.

"Don't get too excited," says Louis.

"I don't even know what to call him. Dad?" The word sounds foreign in my mouth. "Father? Papa?"

"Just call him Mary."

"Shut up."

Louis hands me the phone.

"I'll call when I'm ready," I say.

Toward evening, I finally punch in the numbers. The phone rings five times in Pasadena, then the answering machine picks up. The resident's voice is deep, Midwestern, familiar. *Hey, this is Jim and Laszlo,* he says, *Give us a holler and we'll call you back. Thanks!* I hang up fast without leaving a message.

I try again a few hours later, then twice more, fearing each time that he'll pick up the phone, relieved and sorry when he doesn't. After Louis threatens to leave a message himself, I call a fourth time and ask Pasadena Jim to call me back collect as soon as he can on a very important matter.

The phone doesn't ring the next day. Or the next, or the one after that. I'm hanging from tenterhooks. I can't bring myself to leave the house, yet convince myself that he'll never call. Clearly, Pasadena Jim panicked when he heard my voice and wants nothing to do with me. I should have ignored Sullivan's strategy and written first to let my father get used to the fact that I'd found him. Now, I'm sure he's flown the coop.

The following morning, I call the number one last time and leave a far more detailed message, reminding him that I'm his son. "If you don't want to talk to me, at least have someone else call me back. Please." My desperation is hard to miss.

· thirty-nine ·

He calls the next afternoon.

"This is Jim Matousek," he says.

I know the voice.

"Dad?" I say. "Is that you?"

"Mark?"

"It's me, Dad."

"I'm not your father."

I look out at the dinosaur mountains. A bird is sitting on Louis's poppies. The lightning rod's fallen off of the roof. For a second, I can't talk.

"You have to be."

"I'm not," he says.

"But I have proof."

He chuckles. "Oh, really?"

"Really."

"I don't think so," he says. The man tells me, in a pleasant voice, that he's never been married or had any children. He tells me he wishes he could help me. I open my mouth but no words come out. Louis is sitting on the floor, shaking his head, looking dubious. Finally, I say that I'm sorry I called and didn't mean to bother him.

"No bother at all," he says cheerfully. "Understandable mistake."

"Yes."

"Strange things happen in this world."

"Yes. That's true. They do," I say.

"Things you can't explain," he says.

The bird jumps off the lavender flowers.

"By the way," I ask. "What color are your eyes?"

"Hell if I know," the old man says. "Blue, I think."

"Not gray?"

"I'm color-blind, son," he says.

"So am I," I say.

"Isn't that a coincidence?" he says.

"Isn't it?" I say.

"Well, I guess that's it then. Good luck to you."

"And you," I say.

I hang up the phone with a lump in my throat, unsure of what just happened.

I call Belle to report the news. "We did the best we could," I say.

"Like hell we did." Now and then Belle reminds me of Mom.

"Sorry," I say.

"But what if it's him?"

"It's not," I say.

"How do you know?"

"What's the difference? He's not interested."

"You probably scared him."

"Then who the hell wants him anyway?" I ask.

"Give me the number. I'm calling."

"You're not. It's over."

Belle sounds weepy. I tell her to please let it go.

"I'm not as good at that as you are," she says, making it sound like an accusation.

"I tried!"

"I know."

We hang up the phone feeling tense and distant.

Mac Sullivan is furious. "It's absolutely impossible," he says.

"Maybe," I say, too exhausted to argue.

"This is a slippery scumbag," he says.

"He sounded like a very nice man."

"The odds," says Sullivan, "are a million to one."

"We'll never know for sure," I say.

"We sure will!"

"I'm finished, Mac."

"You can't be finished. The thing's not over."

"It is for me."

"You can't stop now."

"This is as far as I want to go."

Sullivan snorts into the phone. "I hate to lose," he tells me.

"You didn't," I say. "I did."

Sullivan tells me to reconsider, certain that something here *just isn't right*. To placate him, I promise to be in touch should I ever change my mind. Three weeks later, packed up to go home, I leave the detective's memos in a cardboard box in Robert's closet in Santa Fe, believing that I'll never need them again; as a memento, I hold on to Pasadena Jim's address. The last thing we see, pulling out of the driveway, is Gisela and her daughters in cowgirl regalia—matching fringe skirts and fancy boots—yipping and twirling and throwing invisible lassoes around one another in the dust. Gisela hollers and tells us to wait a minute, then takes the huge cow skull off her front gate—big-horned and sun-bleached, a bullet hole through the forehead—and sticks the ghostly thing in my lap.

·forty·

The police tape won't come off of the doorframe; each time I notice the gluey yellow, I think of Sandy on the floor, barely conscious, waiting for help. What did she hear at the moment she died, ear to the floor like a black-and-white seashell? Marie's game shows blaring through the floorboards? The kids next-door playing ball in the garden, traffic horns, the scuttle of roaches, the Tibetan bell swinging outside the window? This place is haunted by so many ghosts now. When I sit on the cushion to meditate, I hear their voices everywhere, crowds of them, whole populations: Marcia murmuring inside her journal, my father humming next to the mirror, Sandy blinking and mouthing for help near the silverware drawer; even the cow skull, which I've now hung over my desk, minding its business, shot through the head and hung up to dry. I have the oddest sense these days of the lines between past and present dissolving, of memory threading time together. They say when you die that your life flashes backward, but this is just short-hand, it seems to me now. Life flashes forward and backward and inward (and upward and downward and outward and through) all the time when you start to wake up; death just quickens and fo-cuses matters, vibrates the colors, helps you see.

When I told my mother about Pasadena Jim, she said, "I told you not to bother." Her lack of sentiment stunned me. I'd hoped, I guess, for some consolation, a moment of mutual, heartfelt closure—perhaps even a hint from her that she was disappointed too, if not for herself then at least for us. But gestures like this are not her style; she knows almost nothing of softening blows, and since the day I reported the results, she's never mentioned the manhunt again.

Strangely, though I've failed to find my father, it's Ida's reac-tion that sticks in my gut. Even today she holds this power, though I've tried to exorcise her from my life. In the limbo years after my father left, she was my abiding fixation; she's the one I missed most of all, hers the ghost that I trailed from room to room, and not the man in the runaway truck. I spent my child-hood hoping intensely that someday my mother would surprise me, emerge from the armor she kept round herself and hold me close without restraint, even though she never could. It was her warmth I craved, her absence that hurt me, her arms I tried to wedge myself into, her touch I craved but couldn't quite capture. The more distant she was, the harder I tried. How strange it is to realize that while lovers' betrayals have long since faded—wounds I thought at the time would kill me—the force of her absence has hardly diminished at all. A man in his nineties, on his deathbed, turned to me once in a hospice where I volunteered and confessed through a wall of cancerous pain that of all the regrets he had in his life, the greatest was losing his mother's love. He was squeezing my hand when he said it. Would I, in his place, have thought the same thing?

The truth I've come to realize is that the night my father came back to get me, I didn't want to leave with him, though sometimes I've imagined I did. I was petrified that he'd take me away, scared to death of losing my mother. Though no child should have to choose between parents—and like any kid I wanted them both—there's no question which of them I would have chosen. In the hard years of living with Ida, I would not have admitted this; I often thought her my nemesis, my ball and chain, and imagined my father to be someone better—the lost, superior half of myself. But that's another fairy tale. He was a stranger to me even then, while my idolized mother was everything—eyes, ears, heart, joy— my measure of being alive in the world. I've wondered sometimes whether hiring Sullivan wasn't, in fact, an unconscious ruse, a play to rouse Ida's sympathy, to draw us closer together. But if it that was my unconscious plan, it certainly backfired miserably. My mother hasn't budged an inch.

·forty-one·

It's early November when Mom calls, a few weeks short of her sixty-eighth birthday. It's mid-week, just after dinnertime. Her voice is hazy, I know something's wrong. She wastes no time with preparation. "Come home if you want to see me," she says. "I'm in trouble."

The following day, after taking the redeye, I'm sitting at Aunt Ruth's kitchen table, holding my breath, looking out the window, waiting for my mother's car to pull up. I know she's about to tell me she's dying; she hasn't looked good in a very long time, and Belle tells me it's gotten worse—coughing fits that keep her from sleeping, loss of appetite, blood in her Kleenex. Whenever I've tried to broach the subject, my mother has shut me up. *When your number's up,* she tells me, *there ain't nothing you can do.* Sitting here now with my eyes on the curb, I'm shit-ass scared, four-year-old scared, like a kid who's never seen dying before. Although I've sat at a hundred deathbeds, washed still-warm corpses at the hospice, tied body bags with twine, faced my own illness for many years, I feel wholly unprepared for this moment and wish that Aunt Ruth hadn't left me alone for the two of us to have privacy. It's the moment of meeting her eyes that most scares me, seeing her fear, knowing that I can't stop it. I brace myself in the chair and wait. The kitchen smells like old ladies and Danish. The oven mitt on the fridge says SHALOM.

When Ida's car appears, I stand and press my face against the screen, straining to catch a glimpse of her. Mom sits behind the wheel without moving, then checks her lipstick in the rear-view mirror and buttons her blouse up to the neck. I know that she's scared of this moment, too—I can feel it—and resist the urge to run out and meet her. I need to have the first look in private, to gather my bearings and fix my own face.

She opens her car door and steps outside. When she turns full front and starts up the driveway, I see that fifty pounds are gone, two-fifths of her body just dropped away. It's like a trick of the eye at first—too extreme to be real. Then I simply want to weep. How can I face her when she looks like that? I take a deep breath, open the door, and step out onto the porch.

Mom stops in the driveway, shakes her head, and holds up the palms of her hands. *This is it*, she says without speaking

"Hi," I say, trying to sound normal. Her shoulders are skeletal when I hug her.

"Not too hard."

"Sorry," I say, then take her elbow to help her up the steps. Mom grumbles and shakes me loose.

"Don't baby me," she says. "I can walk."

Her stubbornness comes as a sudden relief. Even though she's dying, I think, she is still my mother.

In the days that follow, Belle and I try every possible means to coerce her into seeing a doctor, but it's no use. Mom tells us that she's the one who put herself here and she's the one who'll get herself out. She continues to ride the car pool to work, hand out paychecks, make wisecracks, and when she feels like she's going to faint, she curls up for a nap in the ladies lounge. Bruce tries and fails to reason with her. Her boss begs her to stay home and rest, but except for the days when she's too weak to walk, she insists on showing up at her desk as she has for nearly twenty-five years, scaring everyone around her.

Her supervisor calls to ask us to please do something.

"What do you suggest we do?" Belle asks.

"Intervene. Get her help."

"And how do you propose we do that? You know how she is."

"Stubborn as a goddamn mule. It's making everybody crazy!"

Aunt Ruth is at her wit's end as well. With Grandpa in his nineties, Emma too forgetful to leave the house alone, Uncle Marty dead, Shelley and Ronnie out of the state with their own families, she depends on Mom for companionship, even though they've never been friends. "She won't even try!" Aunt Ruth says. "How can she give up like this?"

"She's doing it her way," I say.

"Well, her way stinks if you ask me."

A few years back, I had a dream. Mom was laid out on a table, her naked body divided up like a diagram of a cow in a butcher shop, showing the various cuts of beef. A holy man was dangling a knife point-down over her different parts, showing where she needed healing. In the dream, Mom looked at him calmly and made this strange remark: "Those who have fallen cannot be saved."

"I think she's ready," I say to Aunt Ruth.

"She can't be ready. She's young. She's got grandkids." Aunt Ruth refuses to understand, and it's no use mounting Mom's defense. She's simply being herself, I think, true to form, without consolation. My mother has always been stoical, an enemy of drama and pretense. Now, at a time when most people roll over for doctors, suck up the pity, she simply refuses to play the victim. It's hard to see her suffering—the pain in her chest is terrible—but I'm secretly proud that she's being so headstrong, facing the end with such self-reliance. Watching her struggle to get to her feet, cross the room with unsteady steps, swallow a bite of food she'll throw up, I realize how brave she really is. It makes me proud to be her son.

Two weeks after I arrive, my mother insists that we take a trip to the mall as a family. We try to discourage her but she won't listen. "I'll be laying down long enough," she says as Belle laces up her desert boots. "You don't have to bury me yet."

"Nobody's trying to bury you, Mom."

"Oh, lighten up!" she tells me.

We pile into the van with Belle's boys, Charles, Billy, and Dom, and drive to the local galleria.

"Is this a *mechaya?*" Mom says, fanning the air conditioning down her blouse after the hike from the parking lot. "Isn't this delicious?" When she tilts her head back and gazes up at the waterfall and the tropical plants reaching toward the atrium light, I see that the milky circle around her iris has spread into the brown now, giving her an oracular look. "You like this, kids?"

"Buy us something, Grandma!" says the middle boy, Charles.

"Yeah!" squeals Billy, the youngest, tugging on the leg of her pantsuit.

"Leave Grandma alone!" says Dom, who's fourteen and tries to act cool.

"Little *schnorrers*, I'll buy you!" Mom bends over to tickle Billy under the arms. He screeches and squirms as she holds his face between her hands, smearing orange lipstick from forehead to chin. When Mom straightens up, she starts to cough and can't stop herself for a full ninety seconds. She puts a tissue to her mouth but I see the blood before she can hide it.

"That's enough," Belle scolds the boys.

"I'm fine! This is fun!" Mom says, after she catches her breath. Then she takes my arm and Belle's and walks slowly along the promenade. People stare at her as we pass. She's been to the beauty parlor, put on earrings, makeup, a colorful blouse, but the camouflage only makes Mom look sicker. Belle shakes her head at me.

At JCPenney, she pulls me away from the others; she wants to take me shopping alone. "You know, you dress like a shlump," she says.

"I hate to shop. I hate clothes," I say.

"So be a nudist."

"I wish I could."

"Smartass." We're standing by a rack of plaid rayon leisure

suits. "Your father was a smart dresser. Hoo hoo hoo!" she whistles.

"Really?"

"Oh, yeah. Snazzy. Wow. When he felt like it."

"Can I ask you a question, Mom?"

She doesn't seem to object.

"What did you see in him? Really. Why'd you go and marry this guy?"

"Why?" she asks, examining prices. "Who knows why anyone does anything? I was attracted, I guess."

"Just attracted?"

"Your father had good qualities." Mom's holding up an ugly pair of backless terrycloth slippers. "He used to wear these around the house. You have a pair of these at home?"

The slippers remind me of Fred McMurray. "They're not for me."

"What size do you wear?" she asks, digging through the discounted pile of brown and black footwear. "Your father was a ten."

"Now you remember his shoe size?" I say.

"I remember more than you think."

"Like what?" I ask.

"Like none of your business." She hands me a pair of slippers in black. "A man should be comfortable in his home."

"You sound like Louis."

"I like that boy."

"He likes you, too."

Louis and Mom had met only once, when Louis came with me to Grandpa's ninetieth birthday party. Watching the two of them dance together, I'd realized that they looked something alike—both of them swarthy, dark-haired, and graceful—and that they were alike in other ways, too. Both were earthy, quiet types who hated phonies and refused to perform. Both struggled against depression, were highly sexed and hard to console. Watching the two of them foxtrot together, Mom beaming in her red dress as Louis held her hand in the air, I saw why he seemed so familiar to me from the day we first met in his flower shop, and he asked me, looking shy and scared, if I was free that Friday night—why, in fact, I felt rooted with him. When the dance was over, she kissed Louis on the cheek—like him, she cannot hold her liquor—and knocked the birthday *yarmulke* off his head.

Now, as we move along to the bathrobes, Mom says, "You deserve a *mensch* like that."

"Thanks," I say.

"He's good to you?"

"Wonderful. Better than I am."

"It sounds like me and your father," Mom says. Why is she now suddenly talking about my father so much? "I was never good to your father. He deserved better. I was a selfish bitch on wheels." I've never heard Mom say this before. "He wanted a family but I didn't want him. Chased him away. Then the day he found me with Julie. . . ."

"Found you how?"

"Guess," she says.

"You're kidding," I say.

"I wanted to die, so help me God."

"Where were you?"

"I need to sit down." We take two chairs by the dressing room. "This isn't something you need to hear."

"Yes it is. It really is."

She looks from side to side in case anyone is eavesdropping. "He found us in a goddamn motel. Your father couldn't find a job. It was hard on me, hard on you kids. He said he was going up to Fresno to temp for the day, but that was a lie. He must have already known about Julie but who knows how he tracked us down. All of a sudden he opened the door and there we were."

"What did he do?"

Mom still hasn't looked me straight in the eye. "He came at Julie like a ton of bricks, I thought he'd kill him. Your father was a strong man—skinny but strong as an ox. He picked up Julie just like this. . . ." Mom grips my collar. "He started to choke him against the wall."

"What did you do?"

"I picked up a phone book and whacked him good. Julie's face was turning red. I screamed at your father that I didn't love him. The minute I said it I wished I hadn't. He let go of Julie and turned to me with a look on his face like I'd just killed him." For the first time Mom looks me straight in the eye. "I never saw a man so hurt in my entire life. He didn't say a word to me, just turned and walked out the door. No good-bye, no nothing."

I'm too stunned to be angry. "Why didn't you tell me this before?"

"I wasn't exactly proud," she answers.

"But why did you act like he was so bad?"

"I never forgave him for leaving you kids."

"He didn't have much of a choice, did he?"

"It wasn't just Julie," Mom goes on. "Your father was a lost soul. You want to know the truth?" she asks me.

"I think so," I answer.

"I never should have had you kids."

"Don't say that."

"It's true. But I didn't know any better. I thought a woman had to have kids. Look what I did to your sister Marcia."

"That wasn't your fault."

Mom's starting to cry. "Where was I when she needed me? I was her mother, I should have known."

"Nobody knew," I say quickly, well aware that this isn't quite true.

"You know what your sister said to me once? 'If they find me dead it'll be your fault.'"

"Oh, my God."

"You know what's it's like to live with that every single day of your life?"

I automatically touch her hand but instead of retreating she balls her fingers inside mine. We've never held hands like this before. I'm afraid to move, to scare her away. Her eyes are streaming, lipstick caked at the side of her mouth. I'm aware of people watching us, sitting together, holding hands. Belle and the boys are standing nearby. Mom blows her nose and says, "I never meant to hurt any of you."

"I know."

"I loved you all the best way I could." She has a searching look on her face. "I want you to be happy," she tells me. "Whatever happens, you've got to try."

"I am," I say.

"You're my Rock of Gibraltar."

"I never really knew what that meant."

"It means you get knocked down, you get up and fight."

"I do," I say.

"That's good."

"Like you."

"Not like me." Mom shakes her head. "Don't you ever be like me."

"You're the one who made me strong."

"Not me," she says. "You think so?"

"Who else?"

Mom considers this for a second. "Then maybe I did something right."

After she wipes her nose and eyes, I lead her to the checkout counter. Mom buys me a pair of the ugly black slippers and hands the bag to me, then takes hold of Charles and Billy and lets them lead her toward the toy store, one careful step at a time.

· forty-two ·

I'm sitting by Belle's bed looking at my mother's sleeping face on the pillow, remembering the mornings I'd do this as a boy, following her breaths in the dark, hoping they didn't stop. Watching her now, this tiny skull with flattened gray wisps, I barely hear her breath at all and remember wondering as a child how it would be to live without her, the fear of it and the freedom too, the guilt of ever wishing her dead, wanting the ghosts of anger and heartache lifted. As a child, I'd wonder sometimes, if she were to die, whether my father would reappear to fill the place she left behind.

She snorts loudly and scares me out of my daydream, moaning in her half-sleep, scratching at the neck of her nightgown, trying to untie the knot. "I'll do it, Mom," I whisper, pulling the string free so that she can breathe more easily. Then I take the washcloth from the water bowl, wring it out, and wipe her forehead. At first, this contact was awkward for me; I expected her to push me away, shake herself out of this stupor, demand to know what the hell I was doing. But things have changed these past few weeks; she's grown more docile and wants me to hold her. Now, without opening her eyes, she puts my hand on top of her head, moves it back and forth, telling me she wants to be scratched. I move my fingertips through her hair, and she groans with relief. The medicine seems to make her itch; Mom needs me to be her hands. I sit for hours next to her, touching her arms and neck and feet, watching her breathe in the shade of Belle's bedroom, waiting for signs of pain. I slip splinters of ice between her lips; she sucks at the cold like a cotton-mouthed baby.

Forgiveness comes as a subtle release.

It's hard to resent a person in pain, hard to remember that this frail woman, resting her hollow cheek on my leg, is the same mother I've worshipped and hated. I hardly feel any anger at all, as if the drama has played itself out. I don't know how this has happened exactly. I don't believe in miracle cures, or that people turn virtuous on their deathbeds. I've made no effort to forgive her, but when Mom began to allow me to touch her, an old grudge began to give way inside me—some old squalling grudge hardened into a wall—and the more I touched her, the more the wall softened. Rage and longing, guilt and dread, the hallmarks of our past together, melted into a kind of acceptance, finally into kindness and grief. I'd always prayed that before she died—or when I died, whichever came first—we'd have a time of forgiveness together when we could drop the pain of the past and share the love we kept hidden inside us. It would be like taking a long deep breath together, letting history drop away. Now this seems to be happening. Although my heart is breaking for her, I'm grateful that she's letting me in, grateful for this time together; grateful, too, for something else that neither of us has dared to express. I'm grateful she won't live to see me sick or be forced to bury a second child. I'm grateful we'll both be spared that ordeal, which I've feared at times more than dying itself: imagining the look in her eye when she saw me in bed somewhere, helpless and scared. It's a scene I've rehearsed a hundred times, and each time it's only grown worse in my mind—the guilt I'd feel at watching her suffer, the compulsion to rally and try to protect her when I'd be the one who needed protecting. Perhaps it wouldn't have been that way; perhaps we would have surprised each other. Perhaps Mom would have revealed something new, a motherly warmth that might have helped me. But now, thank God, we'll never know. I put a pillow under her head and turn her face gently toward the window.

Joyce arrives, then Aunt Ruth and Bruce. We take turns sitting shifts beside her. We place yellow pills on top of her tongue, squirt them down with bottled water. Mostly Mom's quiet, curled on her side; other times, she gets terribly restless, struggles onto her hands and knees and crawls around the king-sized bed, like a trapped animal seeking to escape. Her eyes are open but drug-blind. Belle and I block her from falling off the bed while Mom shakes her head and makes angry noises. It's awful to witness the fight left in her, and when Mom finally exhausts herself, she crumples over on her side, hands clenched in front of her chest, like a fetus.

At more peaceful times, Charles and Billy, seven and three, stroke Mom's face and play with her hair, read her stories from picture books. Although she looks frightening, they're not afraid; only Dom, Belle's eldest boy, needs to keep his distance, headphones locked on his head in his room. Bruce and I are entirely civil; he leaves the room whenever I enter, and I pay him the same respect. Sometimes, through the cracked door, I watch him, sitting on the bed beside her, his bald head mottled as an old rock. He's close to eighty-five now, sick himself with multiple ailments, but uncomplaining and kind. He seems to anticipate Mom's sudden needs, and even though I still don't like him, it's touching to watch him being so gentle. It amazes me that they've stayed together, that Bruce didn't let me chase him away in my fit of jealous revenge. Watching him nurse her, it's obvious that something like love has grown between them while I was off making a life of my own. In the end, this may be the point, I think, as he tries to spoon applesauce into her mouth: what truly matters is who sticks around, who won't be chased off, who cares enough to stay through the worst, when the going gets ugly and you need them most. We talk about love so casually, but ask yourself in a quiet moment who will be at your side when you die. Death is the standard that tests life, I think, revealing what's true and who can be trusted; it's the way to know who your true family is. When Bruce eases Mom slowly onto the mattress and pulls the blanket up to her chin, I stay where I am on the hallway floor, moved by the sight of them, and instead of pretending not to have spied, allow him to see me sitting here. Bruce nods at me when he passes by. I hesitate and nod back.

·forty-three·

Twilight time descends on the house, suspending us in waiting. The hours creep by in clockticks and coughs, rustling papers and muted alarms that signal the time for Mom's medication. We move about in slow motion, as if the air itself is syrup, thick with departure as she slips away. I try not to look when Belle wipes her clean, but it's hard not to stare at Mom's naked pelvis. My fascination makes me ashamed, as if I'm breaking some taboo, studying her skin this way, accordion ribs and jutting hipbones, this pale confusion of angles and flesh, but I can't force my eyes away from her. This is the place I came from, I think, where I grew from a random spark of pleasure to a tadpole, and finally a boy, the place where my father laid his ear, where I slid out of darkness into creation. Looking at my mother's taut belly, it seems impossible that I lived here, impossible that I should be dreaming back to how it felt inside that nest, where I heard the world through the folds of her body and floated in her warm black sea. I've spent my life searching for where I belonged, the perfect place in which to feel whole—an optimal fit, an unbroken tie. It's weird to suppose that this longing began with the memory of my mother's body, with this soft helpless shape curled on the bed beside me. Is it possible that the longing that haunts us throughout our lives, and drives us to seek what we seem to be missing, should begin so simply? That just as the soul thrown into creation struggles to find its way back to God, a child struggles to find its way home, in parallel movements of spirit and flesh? Plato called this *anamnesis*—the effort of the soul to remember its source after being thrust into a body—but surely the child mirrors the soul and hungers for a kind of perfection. I think of the golden ball in the fairy tale, lost by the boy who strives to retrieve it—the radiant symbol of past connection hidden just outside his reach, and wonder where this loss begins.

As Belle sponges and dries Mom's skin, powders the hidden spot between her legs, clasps a diaper across her hips, these thoughts wash through my exhausted mind, along with a feeling of sacredness. Belle catches me staring and smiles at me with so much love that her face seems transformed, beatified by devotion and sadness. We're held for a moment perfectly still, with Mom breathing faintly between us.

She dies the next morning without a sound, while I'm still downstairs sleeping. Joyce touches my arm and tells me it's over. I run to the bedroom. Aunt Ruth is sitting in her nightgown next to Mom, weeping, holding her hand; Belle's on the carpet next to the bed, on her knees, sobbing. Mom's eyes and mouth are open, as if she were about to speak. I stare at her face, awaiting a flicker; I touch her head and start to wail. Belle puts her arms around my shoulders, Joyce holds Belle around the waist. We're clasped together like a chain, my face on Mom's breast. We stay like this a long time, clutching one another, moaning out loud, and when at last the emotion subsides, I let go of Mom and look into her eyes, fixed and dark as the eyes of a doll. Where can you be now, I wonder; are you watching from somewhere else? Gently, I close her eyes with my thumbs, lingering to let the skin settle. There are wails behind me, crying kids, but they recede as if outside a chamber. I'm aware only of Mom and myself, and a subtle thing I can hardly describe, a kind of intelligent presence observing, a sort of watching membrane around us registered as a weight on my neck. I've felt this presence before when death happens, the sense it gives of being observed, as if by the one who's passed. I place Mom's hands across her chest and say a silent prayer from the Vedas. *Self is everywhere*, it begins, *shining forth from all beings, vaster than the vast, subtler than the most subtle, unreachable yet nearer than breath, than heartbeat. Eye cannot see it, ear cannot hear it, nor tongue utter it; only in deep absorption can the mind, grown pure and silent, merge with the formless truth. He who finds it is free; he has found himself; he has solved the great riddle; his heart forever is at peace.*

Although she did not find peace in this life, I pray that my mother will find it now. I pray that if second chances are real, she'll come to acknowledge she's more than a body, more than memories, senses and woes, failures, desires, and longing for love, but also a soul in a world full of souls, struggling and free in the very same moment, circling through suffering toward their perfection. I pray that she'll come to this weapon herself, open this mystic truth like a window, lean out of the darkness where she's been trapped and breathe the crisp air of her own startling nature. I feel two small hands on the top of my head and open my eyes to Billy's face reflected in the bedside mirror. He is watching me with a worried look. I take his hand and squeeze it hard, then lean across the wrinkled sheet and kiss my mother for the last time.

· forty-four ·

There's a thunderstorm over Pasadena the day I pull off the freeway, my nose to the windshield of my rented Geo, a street map
spread out on the seat beside me. Louis, Belle, and Aunt Ruth
have all offered to come with me, but I want to meet Jim Matousek alone. Next to the map is a bag containing the galleys of
the book I'm about to publish, Marcia's journal, an envelope full
of family pictures.

Two years have passed since we buried my mother. Driving
along the freeway today, I could see the cemetery in the distance,
perched on top of a hill. I've visited her grave only once since the
day of the funeral, though Belle tends the site on most weekends.
The funeral left me with some bitterness. I'd given the eulogy to a
mortuary filled to standing room with hundreds of my mother's
colleagues from City Hall, then followed the procession up to the
gravesite. To Belle's and my dismay, a plot had been found for

Mom away from the rest of the family—Grandma Belle, Uncle Marty, Joyce's baby Brian. For reasons no one could quite explain, there was only one plot next to Grandma's, and Aunt Ruth was certain that it was hers. We knew that Mom would never have cared—she didn't want a funeral at all, and would have preferred a simple cremation—but her children did care that even in death she'd remained the family outcast. Against our will, she was placed down the hill among strangers, close to the road, away from the shade trees.

When the casket was lowered into the ground, I helped Grandpa toward the grave to throw the first handful of dirt. He sobbed and shook as he dropped the soil onto the mahogany box, then turned to me and asked, "How could your mother have done this to me?" I bit my tongue, said nothing, knowing that Mom would have laughed out loud to hear this final whine from her father. She would have said something funny and mean to cover the hurt he so often inflicted. I simply guided him back to his lawn chair. After the rabbi completed the service, and the crowds had dispersed to their cars, Joyce, Belle, and I stayed behind with the shovels to fill in a few feet of earth by ourselves, with Robert, who'd flown in from Santa Fe, helping. Paula, my photographer friend, stood at a distance taking pictures. Louis pulled rocks and weeds from the dirt; Billy made circular shapes with gravel at the side of the open grave. When we were too tired to shovel more, we stood gazing into the hole in the ground, not wanting to leave her alone in that place. Finally, we drove away.

I press my face against the windshield, trying to find the street through the deluge. Since the day Pasadena Jim gave me the brush-off, I've fantasized about how it would be to knock on his door and see his face, but the time has never been quite right till now. I needed to finish my book after Mom died, and after eighteen months of concentrated work, I finally delivered the manuscript. With my fortieth birthday around the corner, and publication a few months off, it felt like time to get this over with. Navigating my way through the rain, looking for the address Sullivan gave me, I'm more nervous than I expected to be and, after several wrong turns, finally locate the right street and come to a modest stucco duplex set back behind a fenced-in garden. I pull over to the curb and turn off the engine. The steering wheel's damp from the sweat on my palms.

I see no sign of anyone home, no porch light or car in the driveway, but have promised myself to wait around for as long as this takes. If I have to sit here all day, I told myself, I'm going to meet Pasadena Jim and close this matter once and for all. I smoke two cigarettes in a row, practice smiling in the mirror, chew a very strong breathmint; then I open the car door, step out into the rain, and walk quickly up to the porch. No name is posted on the buzzer or mailbox. I check to see that no one's watching, then peek inside at several pieces of junk mail with Jim Matousek's name on them. So, I think, he hasn't moved. The draperies are closed with no light on inside. The neighbor's dog starts yapping madly. I hold my breath and push the bell.

No response. I ring again. A minute passes and still no answer. I open the screen and knock on the door, first gently, then with a rap, but the house appears to be empty. I cross the porch and push the neighbor's bell, sending the dog into a frenzy, then hear someone mutter behind the door. A magnified eye appears at the peephole. When I wave, the hole snaps shut.

I sit on Jim's porch and wait. Five minutes pass. Fifteen. Twenty. Before I retreat to the car, I push Jim's doorbell one last time. The door cracks open right away.

"Can I help you?" a man asks, his face invisible behind the screen.

"Mr. Matousek?" I say.

"You'll have to speak up, son. My hearing aid is in the shop."

"Are you Jim Matousek?" I ask louder, still unable to make out the face.

"I sure am. Who are you?"

"I'm Mark Matousek," I say. Immediately, the screen door swings open, revealing a pot-bellied man in a stained undershirt and falling-down trousers clipped to a pair of red suspenders. He's about seventy, bald and unshaven, on the short side, with the face of a farmer and bright green eyes. The second I lay eyes on him, I know that he is not my father.

"I remember you," he says. "You're the one who called me up."

I want to turn and walk to the car and never look this way again. "Yes, I am."

"What are you doing here?" he asks.

How can I cut this off right away without offending the old man? "Just passing through."

He smirks, nods. "You thought I was yanking your chain?"

"No," I try to sound emphatic. "Not really."

"I don't blame you," the old man says, "Not in this crazy day and age." He looks at the grim weather over my shoulder. "Hell of a day to go knocking on doors, though."

"I'll go now. I'm sorry. . . ."

"Don't run off yet. I don't get much company." The rain is blowing horizontally, splashing the porch steps and drenching my boots. "I'd invite you in but the place is a mess. When you live alone . . ."

"What about Laszlo?"

"How'd you know about my Laszlo?" Jim Matousek asks with a smile. His Laszlo? It can't be. I tell him briefly about Mac Sullivan and how sure he was that Jim was my father.

"You mean to say you had me tailed?"

"Not tailed," I say. "Just watched."

"Through the window?"

"No, of course not."

"You sure?"

"Absolutely."

"I don't need no Peeping Tom! And he don't need to see what I got!" The old man chuckles. "God almighty."

"No one peeped."

"That's good," he says. "You really meant business."

"I did."

"My Laszlo died two years ago. I buried him out back in a crate."

"A crate?" I say.

"I'll show you a picture." He disappears into the house and for a second I wonder if he's a psychopath, and I'll be the one in the next crate out back. Then he returns with a framed photograph of a cocker spaniel on its haunches, tongue lapping out toward the old man's face. "This was my Laszlo," says Jim Matousek.

"Oh," I say, feeling absurd.

"Two years later and I still miss him. What a good little boy he was. When did you last see your father?"

"1961," I say.

"That's a long time to miss somebody. Must be tough. I never had any kids myself. Hell of a big mistake. Never wanted to be tied down. When you're young, you don't think about getting old or needing anybody. Too busy running around for that. Then you wake up one day in an empty house. . . ." The old man shakes his head. "We make our choices. I wanted my freedom. You sure you don't want a cup of coffee? The place is a mess but . . ."

"I need to get going. But thanks," I say.

"You got any kids?"

"No, I don't."

"It's not too late. You've still got time."

"I don't think so," I say.

"You married?"

"Yes."

"Well, that's good. At least you're not all by yourself."

"I'm not."

"Thank God."

"Thank God," I agree.

"He might still turn up someday," he says. "Don't give up. You never know."

"Well, thanks," I say.

"You're welcome, son."

We shake hands and I sprint out through the rain to the car. I see him through the blurred window, lingering at the door watching me. The old man looks abandoned himself, standing alone in an empty house. I tell myself to drive away, I've got my answer, it's time to move on, but something catches and stops me from moving. My finger is on the ignition key but I can't seem to turn it. Suddenly, a blast of emotion shoots out of me with no warning and has me sobbing against the window. I'll never see my father again. I'll never know why he didn't come back, who he was, where he went, how he lived, what, or if, he thought about me. I'll never have a final answer, no neat closing stitch to this long operation. I've been waiting for someone to come back and save me, give me his blessing, tell me I'm good, for as long as I can remember. Now I know this will never happen. The waiting is finished, there's nobody coming, but along with this sadness I feel something else: relief that the game is finally over. There won't be closure or resolution, just this ragged imperfect moment, full of loose ends and dangling conclusions: a lonely old man standing alone on a porch, a journal whose ripped pages I'll never find, a handful of pictures with missing faces, a middle-aged guy inside a Geo, moaning into a handkerchief. The tears sting my eyes like soap in a wound and remind me of something I saw long ago. I was in Italy watching an artist friend as he restored a Renaissance painting, the image so encrusted by time that it had become invisible. My friend dipped his brush in the lye-smelling liquid and ran it across the grimy surface, revealing an eye, a cheek, an ear, and finally the face of a young boy gazing up at the angel Gabriel. It surprised me that something so foul and evil-smelling could uncover so much hidden beauty, and now, sitting inside my rental car, I wonder if grief doesn't work this way, too, brewing deep inside our bodies, poisonous if withheld too long, but cleansing upon its release. Maybe it's grief that makes a man, leads him to the truth of his life, becomes his blessing in the end.

The Boy He Left Behind

Jim Matousek waves at me, then opens the door and walks into the house. He parts the curtain and looks out at me; seeing him with his hand on the glass, I'm struck by the memory of standing that night with my face to the window, looking out at my father's truck, unable to stop him from leaving. I blow my nose and start the engine, honk the horn once for old times' sake. Then I drive slowly out into the rain.

· epilogue ·

"Put some clothes on!" Louis yells.

Our new apartment is decked out with candles and flowers, a fire's burning, the Empire State Building is lit up gold over the sprawling tops of brownstones. The dog has just gotten out of a bath and is plumped up on the couch like a furry Oreo. Our friends will be here in half an hour to celebrate my fortieth birthday, but I'm still sitting in my bathrobe, looking over these pages I've written, hoping that I've told the truth. I question what telling the truth means, lately, especially as it applies to one's life. *I see the world through the eyes of a fly, a thousand facets of each moment at once.* Pessoa, the poet of many disguises, a man who invented a dozen personae—writing differently as each—wrote those words fifty years ago, and might have been speaking for anyone who thinks too much and trusts too little. Like him, I see the world from too many angles for any one version to appear wholly true. Too much is always left out in the choosing, and choice will always distort what happened. But how else can you tell a story? You hope that the choices cohere somehow, create at least a semblance of truth. You hope that, against the odds, you've succeeded. Tonight, I'm not at all sure that I have.

"Five minutes," Louis shouts from the bedroom. I put these pages away in my desk and look around in utter amazement: that I survived to buy this place, that Louis has stuck with me through the bad times, that we've been given our futures back without our having been sick at all. Six months after returning from Pasadena, I found a doctor with passion and faith, and the coming treatments he promised now seem to be working for both of us. One day last spring, we walked down to the Bowery and bought each other gold bands with secret inscriptions on the inside. Seeing that wedding ring scared me at first—I didn't know how long I could wear it, still thinking that I was hard-wired to run away—but I'd always wanted to marry someday, to put down roots and make a home. I'd wanted to prove my parents wrong, to turn their story upside down. I'm not declaring victory yet, but the signs are remarkably hopeful.

Finally, the doorbell rings and my ten best friends pile in with gifts and bottles. Toasts are made. Barbara stands up and clinks my glass. Joe puts a white rose in my lapel. They give me a Buddha with half-closed eyes, and more Champagne than I can drink sober. Then we dance like there's no tomorrow.

· acknowledgments ·

This book could not have been written without the inspiration, indulgence, and blessed goodwill of Susan Petersen Kennedy, Joy Harris, Barbara Graham, Cindy Spiegel, Robert Levithan, Florence Falk, Joe Dolce, Jim Mullen, Paula Allen, Eve Ensler, Ariel Jordan, James Lecesne, Samuel Kirschner, Michael Klein, Gary Lennon, Marie Howe, David Deutsch, Patrick Lewis, Deborah Treisman, Katharina Tapp, Mary South, Hugh Delehanty, Sue Grand, Robby Stein, Amy Gross, Mark Epstein, Ken Wilber, Marcia Lippman, Cynthia O'Neal, Amy Hertz, Judith Hirsch, May Wong, Leslie Daniels, Kassandra Duane, Erin Bush, Howard Morhaim, Jennifer Hershey, Paul Bellman, M.D., Jim Curtan, Anne Simpkinson, Ram Dass, Toinette Lippe, Sally Fisher, Rusty Unger, Dan Wakefield, Ruth Kaplan, Belle Blechen, Charles and Billy Blechen, Dominic Estrada, The MacDowell Colony, Three Lives & Company, and Heartbeat Records.

To each of you, my deepest thanks.

And to Louis Morhaim, most of all, who moves through the world with kindness and love.

·about the author·

mark matousek is the author of *Sex Death Enlightenment*, an international bestseller that was nominated for two Books for a Better Life awards, and co-author (with Andrew Harvey) of *Dialogues with a Modern Mystic*. Educated at the University of California, he is a former senior editor at *Interview* magazine, and theater critic for Reuters International, whose work has appeared in numerous anthologies (including *Wrestling with the Angel*, *The Good Life*, and *In the Company of My Solitude*) as well as *Harper's Bazaar*, *Details*, *The New York Times Magazine*, *McCalls*, *Vogue*, *Common Boundary*, *Yoga Journal*, and *The Village Voice*. Nominated for a National Magazine Award in 1993, he lives in New York City.